Luftwaffe X-Planes

German Experimental and Prototype Planes of World War II

Luftwaffe X-Planes

German Experimental and Prototype Planes of World War II

By Manfred Griehl

Greenhill Books,
LONDON

Stackpole Books,
PENNSYLVANIA

Greenhill Books

Luftwaffe X-Planes: German Experimental and Prototype Planes of World War II
first published 2004 by Greenhill Books, Lionel Leventhal Limited,
Park House, 1 Russell Gardens, London NW11 9NN
info@greenhillbooks.com www.greenhillbooks.com
and
Stackpole Books, 5067 Ritter Road, Mechanicsburg, PA 17055, USA

British Library Cataloguing in Publication Data
Luftwaffe X-planes: German experimental and prototype planes of World War II
1. Germany. Luftwaffe – History 2. Germany. Luftwaffe – History – Pictorial
works 3. Research aircraft – Germany – History. 4 World War, 1939-1945 –
Aerial operations, German 5. Research aircraft – Germany – History – Pictorial
works 6. World War, 1939-1945 – Aerial operations, German – Pictorial works
I. Title
623.7'46'0943'09044

ISBN 1-85367-577-6

Library of Congress Cataloging-in-Publication date available

Design by www.mousematdesign.com

Contents

Luftwaffe X-Planes
German Experimental and Prototype Aircraft of World War II

Preface

The development and evaluation of German prototype and experimental aircraft was largely carried out by the various German aircraft manufacturing companies at their own private airfields. All of the major German aircraft producers also employed their own skilled pilots, although these pilots typically boasted the technical know-how of an aeronautical engineer. A pilot such as this would be termed a *Flugzeugbaumeister* or aircraft master engineer. Only after passing the first stage of flight testing under company supervision by the local *Einflugbetriebe* (aircraft testing team), was a prototype experimental aircraft handed over to the Luftwaffe. After the initial testing of each of the major parts of an aircraft, typically the airframe, the engine(s) and installed ancillary equipment, new machines were tested by the *Kommando der Erprobungsstellen*, or KdE (Evaluation Sites Command), which itself fell under the command of the *Reichsluftfahrtministerium*, or RLM (Reich Air Ministry). Under the auspices of the KdE, several Luftwaffe evaluation sites were established to fulfil specifically the roles of testing the various parts (as above) of any new aircraft. After passing comprehensive tests, a new aircraft, together with its prototypes or pre-series aircraft, would be dispatched to an evaluation unit (or units), designated as either an *Erprobungskommando* (Evaluation Command) or an *Erprobungsstaffel* (Evaluation Squadron). Full test documentation accompanied these aircraft describing both the type's tactical performance and its technical parameters.

Early years of aircraft evaluation in Germany

Following the dissolution of the German aviation industry after the end of World War I, Germany's former aircraft producers (and a few new ones) commenced, in secret, the design and development of new aircraft types *without* the permission (permission being required) of the Allied authorities. At first, only small single-seat fighters were constructed, these being built in rather small quantities. Later on however, medium and heavy bombers such as the Dornier Do11 and the Do13 were developed and handed over to Lufthansa and other civilian firms, disguised as large transport aircraft, in order to gain these firms' help in carrying out a long-term evaluation.

During the growth period of the new German air force between 1935 and 1945, it became necessary to evaluate many aircraft designs in all categories, ranging from small one-engined- to powerful six-engined aircraft as produced by the various German aircraft manufacturers. Many new types were developed in Germany during the period of relative peace preceding World War II, yet because German resources, even then, proved to be limited, it was ordered by the RLM that a small number of prototype aircraft, typically three, were built by the various firms bidding for the same contract. As an example of this, the development of a prototype heavy four-engined bomber as offered out to Dornier and Junkers (amongst others), resulted in a contract to manufacture only a small batch of Do 19s and Ju 89s. Inkeeping with RLM practice, all of these developments were tested both by the various aircraft producers and the Luftwaffe evaluation sites simultaneously. Before 1935, the responsibility for and organisation of aircraft development and testing was veiled in secrecy, using special designations for the various new aircraft designs taking shape at German airbases, or indeed moving development abroad to places such as Switzerland, Sweden or the USSR. While Dornier tested new aircraft at Altenrhein near

the Swiss shores of Lake Constance for example, Junkers worked on new combat aircraft in both Sweden and Russia. Other military designs, especially those for long-range land- and sea-based aircraft, were produced by Dornier or Rohrbach at Italian and/or Danish production sites.

Furthermore, at a secret test site at Lipetsk in the USSR, aircraft research and development was jointly undertaken by the aviators and engineers of the USSR and the German *Reichswehr*. Because the Treaty of Versailles did not allow Germany to develop its own military aviation industry after the end of World War I, the German Supreme Command asked for Russian assistance. The Russians, for their part, were looking for both new techniques in air warfare *and* modern combat aircraft with which to equip the Red Army. With no influence or interference from the Inter-Allied Control Commission, the USSR and Germany planned to issue any aircraft jointly developed to their respective tactical training units – to the Red Army in Russia's case and, in Germany, to the secret military flying organisation under the command of the *Reichswehr* (the German army from the end of WW I to 1933). During the summer of 1921, the Germans tried to produce powerful single- and twin-engined combat aircraft capable of carrying out both day- and night-raids. Several types of Junkers aircraft were tested by the German authorities in Russia. A so-called flying school was established in Russia, tasked with carrying out frontline evaluation of new military types of German aircraft, far away from the prying eyes of controlling Allied officers in Germany. The first attempt at this frontline testing of new types was begun in the summer of 1928. Virtually all German designs capable of military use, such as new bombers, were transported to Lipetsk. For example, the Rohrbach RoVIII *Roland* was flown to Russia and tested as an auxiliary bombardment aircraft, but with only limited success. Additionally, smaller aircraft, for example the HD 38 and HD 45, the Heinkel He 59 and

Do F (Do 11) and Do P, were brought to Russia and evaluated under simulated combat conditions by German pilots and crews, before the final closure of the *Reichswehr* flight test centre at Lipetsk in August 1933.

From 1933, only very few German aircraft development and testing establishments remained abroad, these being in southern and northern Europe. However, at this time a wholly new organisation was established to fulfil aircraft evaluation and testing on an altogether larger scale than before. This work was to be undertaken by the *Erprobungsstellen der Luftwaffe (*Evaluation Sites of the Luftwaffe) based all over Germany.

Erprobungsstelle Rechlin

An aviator test- and training institute had been established at Rechlin on Lake Müritz in 1916. On 29 August 1918 the *Flieger Versuchs- und Lehranstalt* (Aircraft Trial and Test Station) Rechlin was established under the designation *Kommandant der Flughäfen* (Officer Commanding, Aifields) *Müritzsee* under the command of *Hauptmann* (Captain) August Joly. Up until 11 November 1918 (the end of the First World War), this new evaluation unit tested all new aircraft and equipment.

New but secret flight testing activities were recommenced in 1922. Early in 1928 the existing buildings at Rechlin were taken over by the *Albatros Flugzeugwerke* (aircraft factory) *GmbH*. Additionally, a few more hangars were constructed and used by Albatros. From 1928 onward, all facilities at Rechlin were steadily and regularly enlarged to fulfil the many new tasks required of this secret evaluation site; several more hangars were built from 1929, for example. With the exception of the BFWM22, nearly all new German aircraft developments were sent to Rechlin for evaluation. Despite many evaluation flight crashes, it succeeded in selecting those aircraft, from the many designs which could have fulfilled the demands of the *Truppenamt*, used to arm what was to become the future Luftwaffe. On

1 June 1931, the *Erprobungsstelle* of the *Reichsverband der Deutschen Luftfahrtindustrie* (Reich Society of Aircraft Manufacturers), or RDL, situated at Staaken and Rechlin, was split into five separate departments, of which the major two were those used for the testing of new aircraft and new aircraft engines. The others evaluated new wireless systems, other ancillary equipment and were involved in problem solving in other aviation matters, such as aerial photography. The RDL was ordered by the *Truppenamt* (Army Office) of the *Reichswehr* to continue with its secret development of German military aircraft as ordered in the autumn of 1929. In 1932, several transport aircraft were tested to examine if they would be capable of use as auxiliary bombardment aircraft. Besides the Ju G24 and Ju 52, the Dornier *Merkur* (Mercury) and Rohrbach Ro VIII were evaluated as part of this program. Additionally, the first batch of fighters including the He 51 and Arado Ar 65 was tested here.

On 30 January 1933, important proposals were put forward concerning an enlarged facility at Rechlin for the development and testing of new aircraft. On the back of this, a new military airfield at Lärz (near Rechlin) and subsequently the *E-Hafen* at Roggentin nearby were established by the new Luftwaffe command, both to accommodate the testing of aircraft and ancillary equipment.

By 1936, a huge Luftwaffe evaluation site had evolved, incorporating several engine testing sites. Buildings for officers and specialists were built around the main airfield near Ellerholz, east of Rechlin. In addition, a row of huge hangars was erected together with a widespread refuelling system and an ammunition dump, just east of the small village of Rechlin proper on the shore of Lake Müritz. Also engine test beds, a power station and the control tower were all built, followed by a second tower a short time later, again constructed near Lake Müritz. Subsequently, near the evaluation site itself, several smaller houses, called *Siedlung* Rechlin, were built to house officers and engineers working at the Rechlin evaluation centre in order that they should not live too far from their work!

On 9 November 1934, a secret exhibition was staged at Rechlin presenting the He 45, He 46, He 70, Ju W34, Ju 52 and Do 11. which were all shown with ancillary equipment fitted.

Then in 1935, a new German Luftwaffe was officially established. During the course of that year and the following year, many brand new combat- and training aircraft, especially the first Bf 109, Do 17, Hamburger Flugzeugbau Ha 137, Henschel Hs 123, Hs 126, He 111, Ju 86 and Ju 87, were sent to Rechlin to undergo their first Luftwaffe evaluation.

On 22 May 1936, an impressive exhibition was held at Rechlin showing not only the Ju 86, the He 111 and the Do 17 bombers, but also the He 112 and Fw 159 fighters together with many more improved types. Beside the *Reichsminister der Luftfahrt* (Reich Minister of Air Transport) and *Oberbefehlshaber* (Supreme Commander) of the Luftwaffe, Hermann Göring, the *Reichskriegsminister* (Reich War Minister) von Blomberg together with several other high-ranking officers were present. A few weeks later, on 10 July 1935, the same aircraft were inspected by Adolf Hitler himself.

In 1937, still more new prototypes went to Rechlin; beside the Messerschmitt Bf 110 destroyer, engineers at Rechlin commenced their evaluation of one of the new Ju 88. Furthermore, the Fw 57 and a few Henschel aircraft, notably the Hs 122, Hs 124 and Hs 127, were intensively tested there. During the course of 1937, six new aircraft crashed at or near the site, killing 18 members of the Rechlin evaluation team. However, despite all the dangers associated with the evaluation of new aircraft types, it was viewed as simply too important a task to stop the program at this stage.

In 1938, increasing numbers of improved variants of the combat aircraft expected to enter Luftwaffe service arrived at Rechlin. Most of them were prototypes of the Bf 109

and He 111, but there were also some new designs such as the Ha 141, later designated the Blohm & Voss BV 131, the Ar 198 and even a few more experimental types found their way to Rechlin at about this time. Additionally, the first Do 217, more than just an improved Do 17, became ready for testing as the third two-engined bomber earmarked for service with the Luftwaffe. Simultaneously, the Ju88 was tested as a heavy dive-bomber armed with special weapon loads.

In 1939, all aircraft evaluation was placed under the command of the *Generalluftzeugmeister* (Officer In Charge, Aircraft Procurement) who was responsible for the *Technisches Amt* (Technical Office) of the RLM, and who was also responsible for all other evaluation sites. Despite new responsibilites given to the various departments within Rechlin, flight tests were still carried out in the usual way. Another important aircraft reached Rechlin that year: the first Focke-Wulf Fw 190. In addition, the Fl 265, the Hs 128 V1 and the Me 210 V1 were all tested by pilots at Rechlin.

During 1940, beside the Fw 190 and Me 210, a new four-engined bomber, the He 177 V1, arrived at Rechlin, to be tested intensively by the evaluation team. Many technical problems were found during the evaluation of these types, though not all of the issues could be resolved by the Rechlin staff due to shortened development time constraints of the Me 210 and the He 177 in particular. At about the same time Rechlin succeeded in testing Fw 190s fitted with the first of the BMW 801 radial engines which would be used to replace the less powerful BMW 139s in the then not-too-distant future. To improve existing fighter power, variants with larger aircraft engines were sent to Rechlin; several new Bf 110s were evaluated in 1940, together with the first prototypes of the new Bf 109F and the first pre-series Do 217.

As of 1941, evaluation tasks were expanded once more; the development of the large He 177 bomber involved much work in order to obtain a reliable aircraft finally capable of front line service.

After the outbreak of hostilities, theatres of war became increasingly large, close air support becoming increasingly important for the Wehrmacht ground units fighting on long fronts, often without powerful enough weapons and enough supplies. Therefore it became an important task for the *Erprobungsstellen* to test the first Hs 129s, as well as special ground attack variants of the Fw 189 and the early Fw 190 fighter/bomber.

At this stage of the war it became obvious that German air transport capacity was too limited to fulfil all its necessary tasks over the European war theatre *and* the north African desert. Therefore, new huge gliders were constructed which underwent test and evaluation activities in 1940. Beside the Gotha Go 242, far larger types such as the Ju 322 and the Me 321 *Gigant* (Giant) were evaluated, although only the Go 242 and a motorised variant of the Me 321, the Me 323, actually passed evaluation at the time.

Month by month, new variants of all the more common combat aircraft were transferred to Rechlin for evaluation. In 1941 and 1942, Rechlin pilots not only flew the newest Bf 109s of the early G-series, but also the improved Bf 110 aircraft of both the F- and G-series and yet more Fw 190 variants. Simultaneously, more powerful bombers were brought to Rechlin. Most of these were prototypes of the Do 217-K and –M, being powered by BMW 801Ds and DB 603As respectively. At the time there were insufficient resources for the Reich to produce four-engined strategic bombers, such as the Allies' Fortress or Lancaster. Therefore those types already in service, such as the He 111 and Ju 88, were continuously improved to allow missions under more difficult conditions during the defence of the Reich, for example under heavier AA fire and against the increasingly potent fighters of the Allies. By the middle of the war, the Luftwaffe was demanding the introduction of heavier destroyer aircraft types to defend Reich territory both by day and by night. Prototypes

of these well armed aircraft, such as the Do 217N and Ju 88C, were sent to Rechlin for testing and evaluation. Later in 1942, the first Ar 240 and He 219 *Uhu* (Owl) prototypes were available and, as usual, were first tested by their manufacturers before being handed over to the various *E-Stellen*. Also, various new transport aircraft became available for testing at this time. Besides the Go 244, a motorised glider, the Ju 252 and Fi 256, both German liaison and transport types, were to start their evaluation phase. However, only a limited number of each were produced due to the lack of sufficiently high quality raw materials.

Rechlin's role was however not limited to German aircraft, several captured aircraft being sent to the site for evaluation. All over German-held territory, teams of specialist engineers were responsible for the recovery of any allied aircraft shot down or forced to land. Those allied machines suffering only limited damage were of tremendous interest to these men, who were also responsible for the recovery of undamaged spare parts from similar aircraft, thus allowing the Rechlin specialists to repair damaged enemy aircraft for comparative flights with German types.

From 1942 onwards, numerous photo-reconnaissance aircraft of the RAF attempted to probe the secrets of the Rechlin test centre. All unrecognised aircraft or those unknown to the reconnaissance specialists back in the UK were labelled "Rechlin #". For example, "Rechlin 104" photographed on 28 June 1943, was possibly the first Ar 232 to land at the airfield. Photos of various heavy night fighter prototypes and new Do 217 variants then being tested at Rechlin were also brought back to England at around this time.

The war visited the *E-Stelle* Rechlin itself early in 1944, when Allied P38s hit hard at Rechlin-Lärz and destroyed a few of the prototypes dispersed around the second evaluation airstrip at the base. On 24 May 1944, a total of 13 four-engined bombers of the 388th Bomber Group appeared over Rechlin-Lärz and dropped 31 tons of bombs although they failed to hit even one of the prototypes located there.

Despite these attacks, the pilots, engineers and men continued with their work to create new weapons for the Luftwaffe. Between May and August 1944, reconnaissance aircraft of the RAF located the first Ar 234 and Ju 287 types, together with a few Me 262s based there. Overwhelming allied air power had not been significantly hindered from reaching their targets all over Europe by the then available German piston-engined fighters or destroyers. Therefore German aircraft manufacturers were ordered, within the shortest period of time, to construct well armed jet fighters and bombers to prosecute a new kind of defensive and offensive air war against the Allies. Not only was the Me 163, a small rocket-powered point-defence fighter, constructed and tested at this time, but also several prototypes of the Me 262 and a few He 280s were evaluated, both in Bavaria and at other sites all over the Reich.

On 12 and 13 June 1944, the *E-Stelle* Rechlin presented a complete review of all the various prototypes then being tested. Beside the huge He 177 (the B-5-prototype), the fast Ju 88S-3, the He 219 and the new Focke-Wulf Ta 154 *Moskito* were shown. Furthermore, all the new major fighter variants and conversions were flown or shown at the event. Beside the Ar 234, Me 163, the new Do 335 and the Me 262, there were also examples of the latest captured Fortress, Liberator, Lightning, Mosquito and other Allied types shown.

On 25 August 1944, Rechlin was again hit, this time by 179 bombers of the US 8th Air Force. There *was* damage to the base this time but it still managed to function, although unlike the previous raid a few prototypes were lost or damaged. Late in 1944, the evaluation of German jet aircraft projects was continued with great vigour. Specialist teams worked on the He 111H which was needed for airborne release trials of the V1. Additionally, desperate attempts were undertaken to use manned V1s, code-named *Reichenberg*, to destroy more important targets through the use of suicide attacks, but on 15 March 1945 all work on this particular weapon was ceased.

Meanwhile, in January 1945, the Red Army had advanced faster than estimated after the *Heeresgruppe Mitte* (Army Group Centre) had been severely mauled and had practically broken down. To stem the Russian ground forces' advance, all available aircraft were required, including those at Rechlin. The inventory of *E-Stelle* Rechlin at the time consisted of both series aircraft and prototypes which was immediately organised into two night bomber *Staffeln* flying the He 111, Ju 88 and Ju 188. Also a fast *Bomberstaffel* (bomber squadron) consisting of nine Ar 234s, two ground attack formations flying the available Fw 190s and two fighter units with a total of 13 Bf 109s and Me 262s were all established. The complete *Gefechtsverband* (Fighting Unit) KdE was dissolved, however, on 19 February 1945, due to serious problems in using prototypes for offensive missions. Also, with Russian ground forces still advancing rapidly, the evacuation of *E-Stelle* Rechlin to Lechfeld in Bavaria began on 24 March 1945.

Once re-established there, the evaluation of the Ar 234, Me 262 and the new He 162 *Volksjäger* (Peoples' Fighter) could start again. Only very few prototypes had been flown from Rechlin to Lechfeld, but that included the first pre-series Ar 234C-3 and some of the He 162s. Meanwhile Rechlin and Lärz were severely hit by American Liberators on 10 April 1945. The last prototypes left Rechlin on 20 April 1945, destined for Bavaria and Northern Germany, the last members of staff of the *E-Stelle* leaving by train on 29 April 1945 before the facilities were blown up by German forces the following day.

Besides the *E-Stelle* Rechlin, several similar units were established across Germany, though they were used for other purposes.

E-Stelle (See) Travemünde

At Travemünde, near the old town of Lübeck and on the shores of the Baltic Sea, the *Reichsmarine* (Reich Navy) had for some time used the island of Priwall for military purposes located there. The facilities of Caspar Werke AG were later expanded and used, from the mid- twenties onwards, for RDL activities. An evaluation site was established there in 1926 comprising an airport usable for both land- and sea-based aircraft. Early in 1928, the facility was used for testing Dornier and Rohrbach flying boats. Although secret military evaluation tasks were carried out there, the site was presented to the outside world as a civilian location, only used for evaluating seaplanes built by the Caspar factory and the testing of civil designs from other manufacturers who lacked sufficient test centres of their own. However, in 1931 engineers tested the He 59 coastal reconnaissance floatplane here, together with the Dornier JII *Wal* (Whale), which were both types destined to become an integral part of German military maritime aviation.

In January 1933, the *Luftschutzamt* (Air Defence Office) of the German Navy took over the command of the former RDL evaluation site at Travemünde and continued work on new but more powerful flying boats and floatplanes. Also, and for the first time, armament tests were carried out here, but in September 1935 a dedicated site for this purpose was established at Tarnewitz.

Beside testing naval aircraft and sea planes, future German day fighter aircraft, some of the most powerful single-seat fighters yet seen at the time, were tested at Travemünde. Beside the Bf 109V1 and -V2, the He 112V1 and -V2 were tested against and compared with the Fw 169V2 and older aircraft such as the Ar 68 and the He 51.

In the summer of 1936, many German maritime aircraft, especially larger seaplanes such as the He 115 or Do 18, were tested on Priwall Island. In 1937, engineers were busy here trying to produce the most reliable long-range reconnaissance flying boat for missions over the sea. Furthermore, trials were carried out to find a reliable means of landing, say, a Fieseler Fi 156 on smaller ships. In 1938, a few He 115 coastal floatplanes were tested

here with the purpose of improving their offensive armament. A short time later, the ship-based Arado Ar 196 appeared together with multi-role combat aircraft such as the Fi 167, which was planned to see service on the first aircraft carrier planned by the German *Kriegsmarine*. Along with the Fi 167, the Avia B324, the Bf 109T and the Ju 87C aircraft were all modified to be used on carriers.

Evaluating autogiros and other helicopters, again for projected use by the German *Kriegsmarine*, took place here. The Fa 330, the Flettner Fl 282 and a few more types were evaluated, to be used, it was planned, as spotter planes from German warships to avoid the attacks of enemy submarines, or as lookouts for sea mines, or for escorting German convoys or single merchant ships. Amongst the last evaluation orders received here were those for the Do 26V6 flying boat and the BV 222C-09 *Wiking* (Viking). Both aircraft, and the Ar 232, were needed to ferry supplies to sites within the Arctic circle.

On 5 May 1945, the evaluation site at Travemünde was handed over by its last commanding officer to British troops, after all aircraft, with the exception of one helicopter, the Fl 282 V20 (CJ+SN), had been destroyed by German forces.

E-Stelle Tarnewitz

Tarnewitz was the base responsible for special trials relating to the armament of nearly all German military aircraft. The site was established near the Baltic coast between the town of Lübeck and Wismar, near the small village of Tarnewitz, but it was not completed until 1938, some time after the first hangars had been constructed. Up to 1944, various machine guns and cannons were evaluated here, as well as several types of weapon turret installed in the more common German aircraft. Furthermore, guided rockets such as the RZ65 or RZ100, as fired from a Bf 109, Fw 190 or Me 210, were tested at Tarnewitz, using old prototypes or damaged aircraft fuselages or wings as targets. Besides these weapons, all kinds of *Werfergranaten* (air-to-air missiles) and also the most effective armament for the Bachem *Natter* (Adder) were drawn up here. Amongst the heaviest aircraft guns evaluated here were the Bordkanone BK7.5, as fitted under the fuselage of the Ju88P-1, or the heavy but recoilless BK8.8. During the last months of the war, several engineers worked on automatic devices and heavy armament for the Ar 234, the Do 335, the Me 262 and other late-war developments.

Another but also important task was the development of anti-tank weapons, especially the use of *Panzerblitz* and *Panzerschreck* air-to-ground rockets, later used in action over the Eastern front.

On 13 May 1944, Tarnewitz was hit by an American low-level attack, which disrupted various trials and evaluations taking place there, even though dispersed around the site. The most important prototypes and experimental aircraft were evacuated shortly before enemy forces entered Tarnewitz, though American forces who captured the site did manage to find the sixth Ju 388 (V6), and in remarkably good condition. Tarnewitz was subsequently taken over by Red Army troops.

Versuchs- und E-Stelle **Peenemünde-West**

The *Versuchs- und Erprobungsstelle* (Testing and Evaluation Site) Peenemünde West was situated on Usedom Island near the mouth of the Peene river and was responsible for the evaluation of rocket-powered aircraft and special weapons. After the first jet- and rocket-powered aircraft produced by Heinkel, the He 176 and He 178 respectively, had been tested, trials were carried out with the Fw 56, He 72 and He 112 types acting as engine testbeds. Later, the first batch of He 111s was tested with rocket-assisted take-off (RATO) propulsion units.

After the DFS 194 rocket fighter prototype had been evaluated, the Me 163 became one of the most important tasks for the engineers working at Peenemünde West. On 2 October 1941, Heini Dittmar flew faster than 1,000 km/h flying a Me 163A prototype. Subsequently the series version, designated the Me 163B, was evaluated.

In addition to this, several rockets and missiles were tested here for the Luftwaffe. The Blohm & Voss BV143 and BV 246 remote-controlled bombs were tested under the wings of Do 217, He 177 and Fw 200 aircraft. Some of the last work undertaken at Peenemünde included the evaluation of the Kramer X-4 air-to-air rocket, planned for use by Fw 190 pilots; work on many ground-to-air AA-missiles; and some concluding work on the Bachem Natter.

E-Stelle **Udetfeld**

In 1940, a testing centre for the various kinds of bombs was established at Beuthen, and named *Erprobungsstelle Oberschlesien* (Evaluation Site Upper Silesia), though in 1941 the place was renamed Udetfeld. Besides all of the more common bombs used by the Luftwaffe, additional types such as those fitted with parachutes were tested here. The site was destroyed by German soldiers in January 1945 due to Red Army forces moving rapidly toward Silesia.

E-Stelle **Tropen**

An *Erprobungsstelle* at Derna in Tunisia was established in order to test all kinds of aircraft and equipment under tropical conditions, with Ju 52, Ju 87, Ju 88, Bf 109 and smaller liaison aircraft all operating from here. Subsequently, both the Fw 190 and Hs 129 were tested here in the Spring of 1943. Following the capture of the region by Allied troops, all personnel together with the remaining experimental types located at Derna were withdrawn back to Italy.

E-Stelle **Süd**

Aerial torpedoes and sea mines were evaluated by the Luftwaffe at their air base at Foggia in Italy. Additionally, bombs were tested at Cazeaux in France, especially those involved in tactical release trials from different altitudes. Besides the Fw 190, He 111 and Ju 88, an exotic prototype, the Do 217PV2 was used for high-altitude bombing trials. After the Allied landings in Normandy and several low-level attacks on the base, the *E-Stelle* at Cazeaux was dissolved on 10 October 1944, the remaining experimental types and series aircraft located there being withdrawn to Germany.

E-Stelle Werneuchen

In April 1942, a special department of the KdE was established at the Luftwaffe airbase at Werneuchen, northeast of Berlin. The main tasks undertaken here included the development of systems for comprehensive naval air reconnaissance, tactical aerial situation determination and perception, the coordination of day and night air defences and fighter/bomber direction for destroying targets from the air.

Work concerning new infra-red target seeking and acquisition devices as well as improvements to existing ancillary aircraft equipment became especially helpful to Germany's air defence. One of the last major tasks at Werneuchen was the final development of the radar for the Ar 234B-2/N, which, it was anticipated, would be applicable also to other German jet aircraft.

E-Stelle Munster-Nord

A top secret test centre was established at Munster-Nord to evaluate all kinds of chemical warfare agents, using a few experimental aircraft fitted with gas-filled canisters. Besides a Ju 88A and –S, a modified Do 217E-3 (KH+CR) was used for evaluation purposes.

Wintererprobung at Dorpat

To obtain reliable information on flying under freezing cold and snow conditions, a small test centre was established at Dorpat. There and indeed elsewhere, several of the more common Luftwaffe aircraft types were fitted with snow skis for evaluation of any performance implications associated with them.

Private aircraft evaluation and testing

Besides the Luftwaffe's own organisation for flight testing and development, several engine and propeller manufacturers were allowed to operate their own military aircraft, experimental types or prototypes for development purposes. Additionally, most of the main engine manufacturers including Argus, BMW, Hirth and Daimler-Benz (amongst others) were equipped with a few experimental aircraft to carry out lengthy tests using brand new or modified aircraft engines earmarked for proposed new aircraft types for the German Luftwaffe. Furthermore, wireless systems were tested in military aircraft handed over by the Reich to companies producing such equipment, including (amongst others) GEMA, Siemens and Telefunken. Last but not least, several manufacturers of ancillary equipment received former experimental types or pre-series aircraft to test their new equipment under flight conditions. Altogether, less than 100 aircraft were operated by German aircraft manufacturers and its delivery firms throughout the Second World War. Much later in the war, most of those aircraft that *had* been allocated to German aircraft manufacturers were subsequently withdrawn and handed back to the Luftwaffe.

1•Above One of the first day fighters for the new Luftwaffe, the Arado Ar 65 was developed in 1931. It was tested early in the thirties together with two Heinkel biplane designs, the Heinkel He HD38 and the HD43, but only with limited success. The type was later replaced by the Ar 68 biplane.

2•Below Only two major variants of the Arado Ar 68 fighter were introduced into Luftwaffe service. A few Ar 68 H aircraft and some other prototypes were evaluated by the Luftwaffe, but were never built in great quantities. This Ar 68 HV1 (D-ISIX) is pictured at Speyer airfield in 1937.

3•Above right One, perhaps two, Heinkel He 45Cs were fitted with the DB 600 piston engine following the rather weak performance of the BMW VI 7.5, as originally installed. It was certainly too weak to reach the performance levels demanded by the Luftwaffe. Since the DB 600s were needed for other aircraft, the engine for this two-seat aircraft was not changed in the full production variants. Some 500 He 45 As and -Cs were produced.

4•Below right The Ar 95, a reconnaissance aircraft fitted with a BMW 132 DC radial engine, was tested as both a sea- and land-based plane. Due to rather poor performance, only the floatplane made it into service, as part of a maritime reconnaissance unit (3./SAGr. 125). Most of the aircraft built were sold to Chile or Spain since there was no interest in the type from the Luftwaffe.

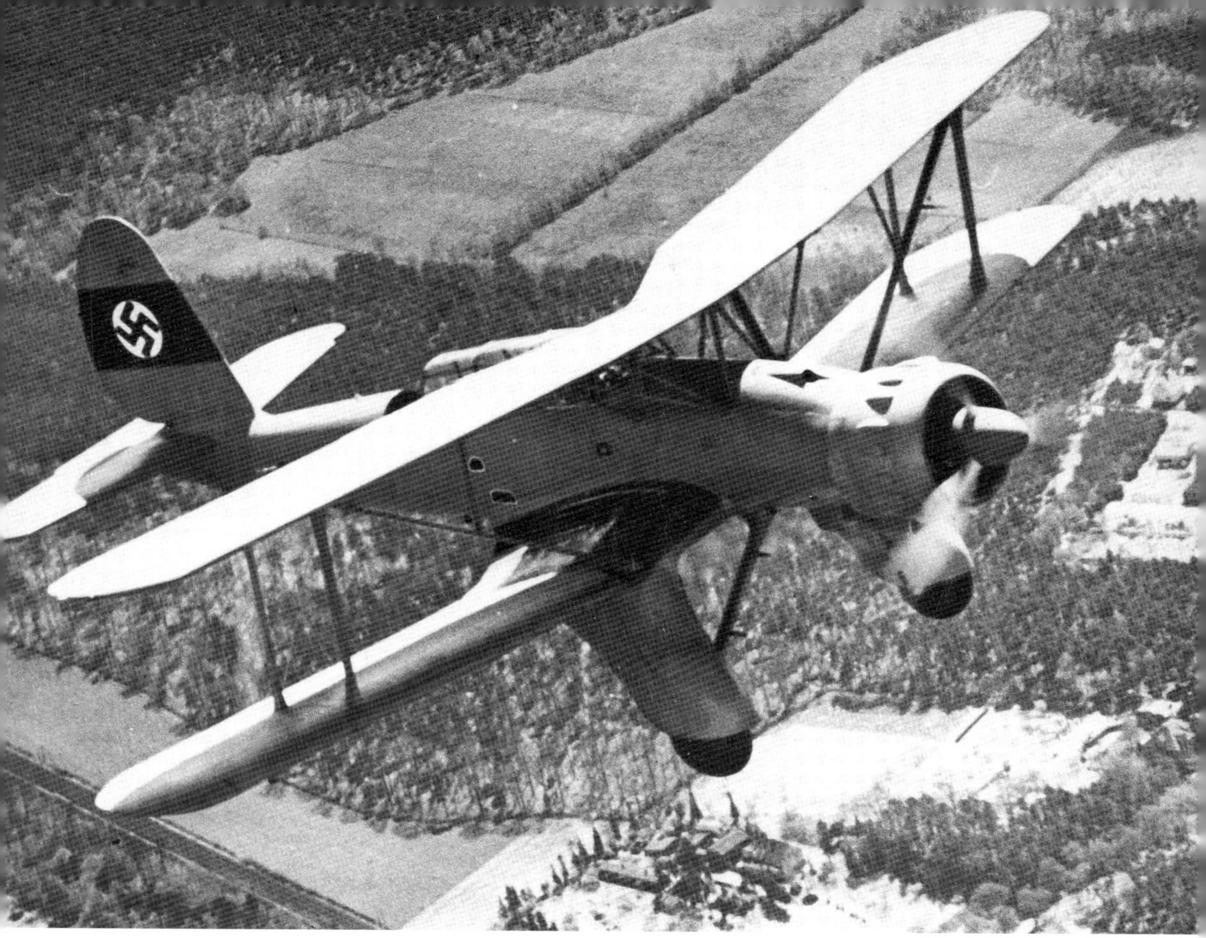

27577

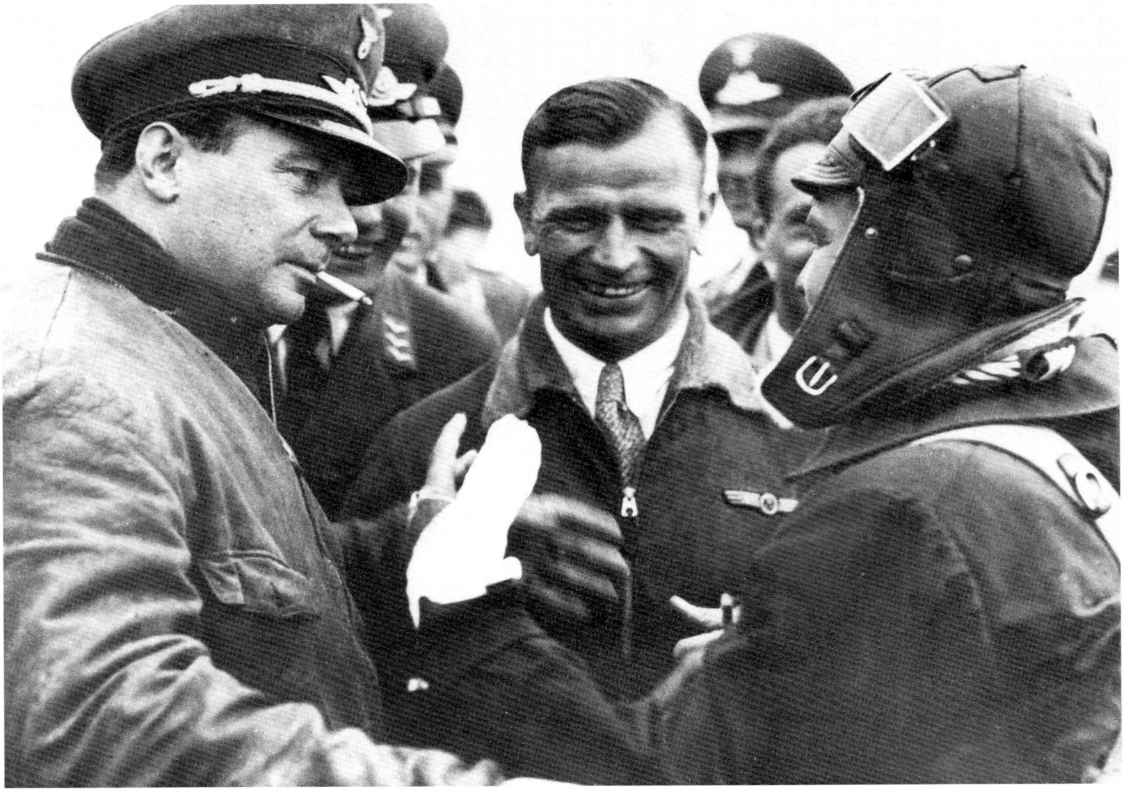

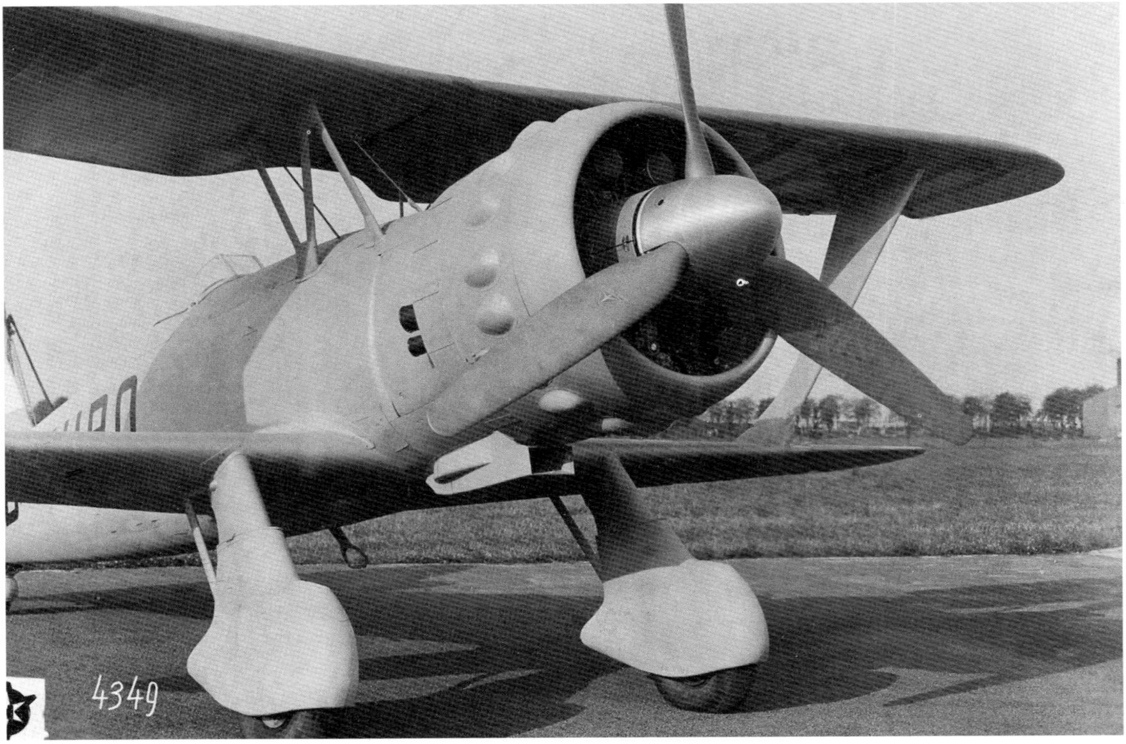
4349

5•Above left During the early growth years of the new Luftwaffe, *Oberst* Udet (left in the picture), later the Commanding Officer of the *Technisches Amt* (Technical Office) of the Luftwaffe, was seen at virtually all Luftwaffe sites at one time or another. This extremely skilful WWI flyer, here shown with the well known air artist Stör, undertook the testing of many new prototypes himself.

6•Below left The role of close air support featured in many different types which were tested by the *Erprobungsstelle* Rechlin near Lake Müritz. The seventh prototype of the Henschel Hs 123 (V7, D-IHBO, production number 0985) was similar to the A-1 version and was fitted with a BMW 132 KV110 experimental radial engine.

7•Above This reconnaissance aircraft, an Ar 198 V1, was built by Arado. The aircraft shown (D-ODLG) was part of a competition and was designed to give splendid low- and high-level performance when operating over the battlefield. It was powered by a BMW 323 A radial engine. A second prototype was manufactured, but the RLM lost interest in the aircraft due to its layout.

8•Below The Hamburger Flugzeugbau Ha 141, later named the Blohm & Voss BV 141, was only tested in small quantities. A number of pilots reported feeling sick when flying this aircraft of so unorthodox a layout largely, it was believed, because the cockpit was moved onto the right wing and not incorporated into the main fuselage. The RLM at this time preferred standard designs only, so there was little chance of the BV 141 making it onto the Luftwaffe's inventory in numbers.

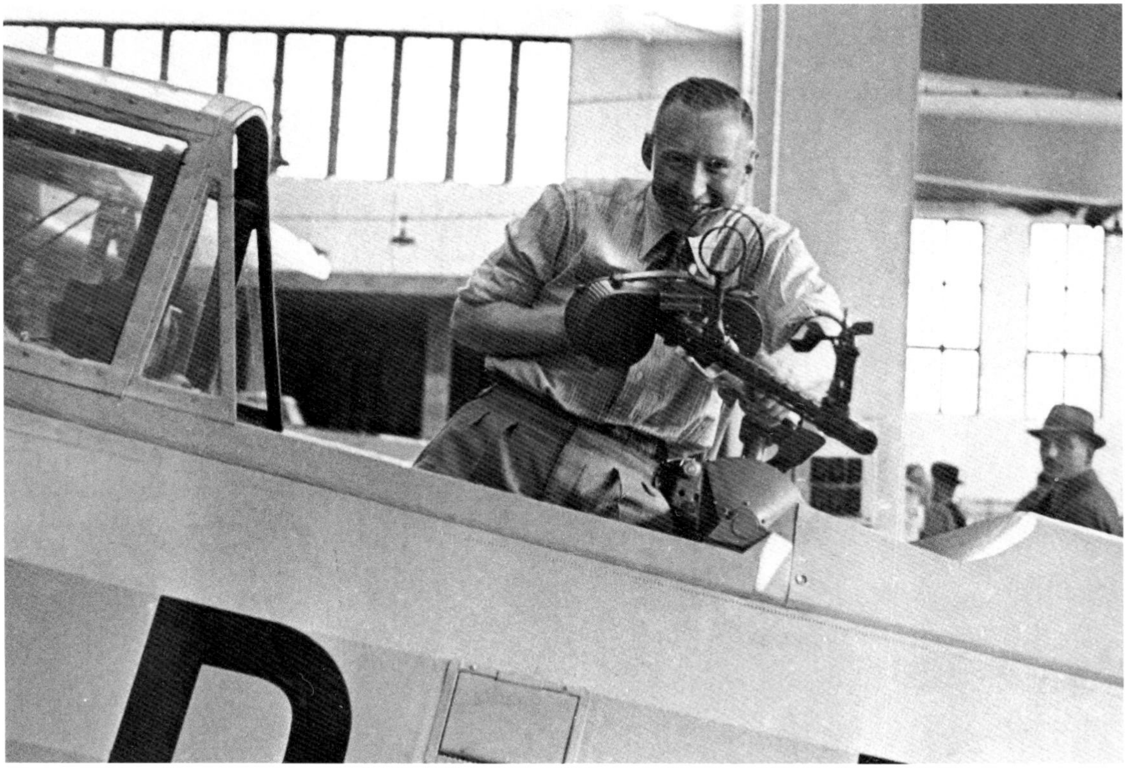

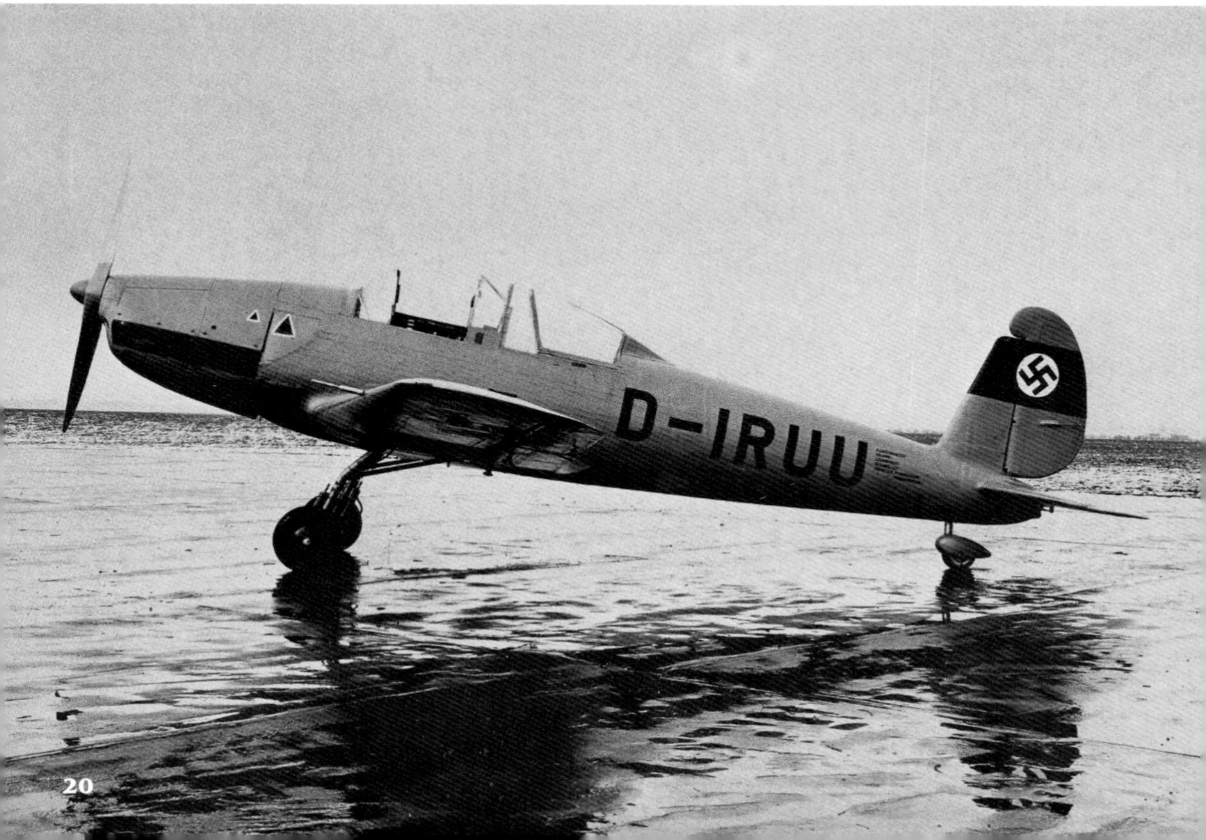
D-IRUU

9•Above left Several regular training aircraft types, such as the Arado Ar 66, Gotha Go 145 and the Ar 96, were fitted with a single MG 15 machine-gun in the rear of the cockpit to evaluate gun types and develop defensive tactics.

10•Below left The first Ar 96 V1 (D-IRUU) was flown with an early version of a completely retractable under-carriage. After numerous tests, it was decided that it was probably better to install a stronger undercarriage since student flyers would lack the skills to effect a soft landing! Note the Ar 96 V1's fairing differed substantially compared with later series aircraft.

11•Above Several different dive-bombers, both light and heavy, were developed by Arado, Blohm & Voss and Junkers before the war. That shown, a Ju 87 V2 (D-UHUH, production number 4922) was flown for the first time on 25 February 1936. This prototype differed from those following in both its cabin fairing and the central fin section.

12•Below In a competition held by the RLM, the Heinkel He 118 competed against prototypes built by Arado and Junkers. The aircraft shown is a He 118 V1 (D-UKYM) which was unarmed and resembled a small He 111. It was fitted with a Rolls-Royce Buzzard engine. Ernst Udet crashed in one of these, following which only a handful more were built.

13•Above Focke-Wulf developed a well-armoured con-version of its highly respected Fw 189 reconnaissance aircraft. The prototype was armed with six machine guns and cannons to support German ground units on the battlefield. However, because the Henschel Hs 129 performed at higher speed and had heavier armament, this particular Fw 189 project was cancelled.

14•Right The third Dornier Do 17 fast bomber prototype (D-ABIH, production number 0258) was powered by two BMW VI D piston engines and was only planned to be an experimental aircraft fitted with 20mm guns. The upper dorsal weapons position was near that later adopted in the full series.

15•Below During the International Flugmeeting at Dübendorf near Zurich in Switzerland, an early version of the Do 17 was flown as a Do 17 K. The aircraft shown (production number 0691) was later recoded with the callsign D-AELE and was used over a long period of time for evaluation purposes. During the competition, the aircraft were maintained by employees from the various manufacturers rather than Luftwaffe personnel.

16•Above The second Ju 88 V2 (D-ASAZ, production number 4942) first flew on 10 April 1937 and was fitted with two DB 600 C piston engines. It was subsequently used for testing the new cockpit section of the planned Ju 288 and later as a training aircraft (VA+EG) by a flying school (FFSC) near Fürth in Bavaria.

17•Above This rare view of the first He 111, initially named the He 111a V1 (D-ADAP, production number 713), shows an early four-seat bomber prototype powered by two BMW VI Ozs, subsequently changed to BMW VI Ds. The aircraft was unarmed for the early phases of its evaluation.

18•Below Three aircraft took part in the so-called Bomber B competition. To compete with the Arado and Dornier designs, Junkers developed the Ju 288, a modern bomber with powerful engines and a heavy defensive armament, with machine guns installed in remote-controlled weapons positions. The aircraft shown belonged to a limited series of Ju 288 C-1 aircraft, produced to replace the He 111 and Ju 88.

19•Above This mock-up of a Fw 191 bomber was also designed and built as a Bomber B competitor and was made out of wood. These mock-ups were built to prove that all instruments and systems installed could be operated by the crew without serious problems caused by cramped conditions in the cockpit.

20•Below The Fw 191 V1 and V2 were first evaluated with two BMW 801C-0 engines installed, since heavier piston engines were not available at the time. The third and fifth experimental types were fitted with two of the rare Jumo 222 double radial engines. However, as Jumo 222s were not reliable enough to be used under war conditions, it was proposed that the engines be changed once more, this time to DB 610s.

21•After it became obvious that Allied production capacity would result in the production of faster and better-armed aircraft, the RLM insisted that improved single seat fighter aircraft were needed in the near future. Several designs had been worked on, but only the Fw 190 had a chance to be built in large quantities. The photo shows the first experimental type, the Fw 190 V1 (D-OPZE).

22•The first Fw 190 V1 was first flown with a BMW 139 radial engine installed, but this was subsequently changed since its cooling proved to be inefficient and more engine power was needed. Therefore, during its evaluation phase, this first Fw 190 was tested with a BMW 801 double radial engine as a replacement.

23•Above The He 112 and the Bf 109 were opponents in the competition for a powerful single-seat piston-engined fighter. Despite the Heinkel design seeming to offer a better prospect of becoming a more powerful and upgradeable fighter over the following years, the RLM believed in Willy Messerschmitt as a more skilled fighter designer than the team used at Heinkel.

24•Below The He 112 V4 (production number 1943) became available in the summer of 1937. This prototype single-seat fighter aircraft was powered by a Jumo 210 C piston engine and was tested under combat conditions during the Spanish Civil War. The aircraft was later used as a test bed for a rocket engine installed in the rear fuselage.

25•Above During the fourth international Flugmeeting at Dübendorf which took place from 27 July to 1 August 1937, *Major* Seidemann (pictured here) demonstrated the impressive performance of the new standard fighter for the German Luftwaffe, the Bf 109 V7. The fourth B-0 aircraft had a high gloss finish over all surfaces and was unarmed to save weight.

26 & 27•Right and Above Right The last series version of the famous Bf 109 was built at the Wiener Neustädter *Flugzeugwerke* (Aircraft factory) in Austria, just south of Vienna. After building a full scale mock-up, the first experimental aircraft was assembled there. There followed a brief analysis of its flight characteristics before the aircraft was sent to Rechlin for further evaluation, to be followed later by full production Bf 109 Ks.

28•Below Right To save precious resources as much as possible, it was decreed by the RLM that metal parts would be substituted by wooden ones. The Hirth Werke therefore tried to construct wings and other major components of the Bf 109 G and K using wooden or indeed plastic parts. Those places where wooden and/or plastic parts met metal components could be extremely difficult to join!

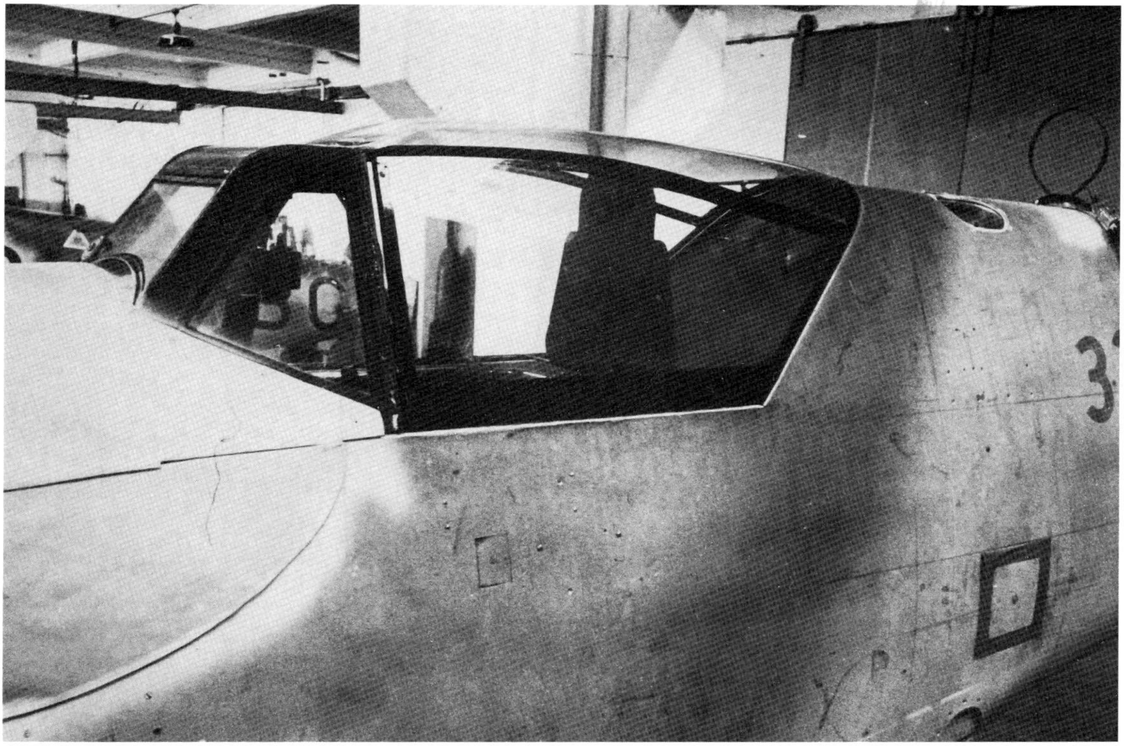

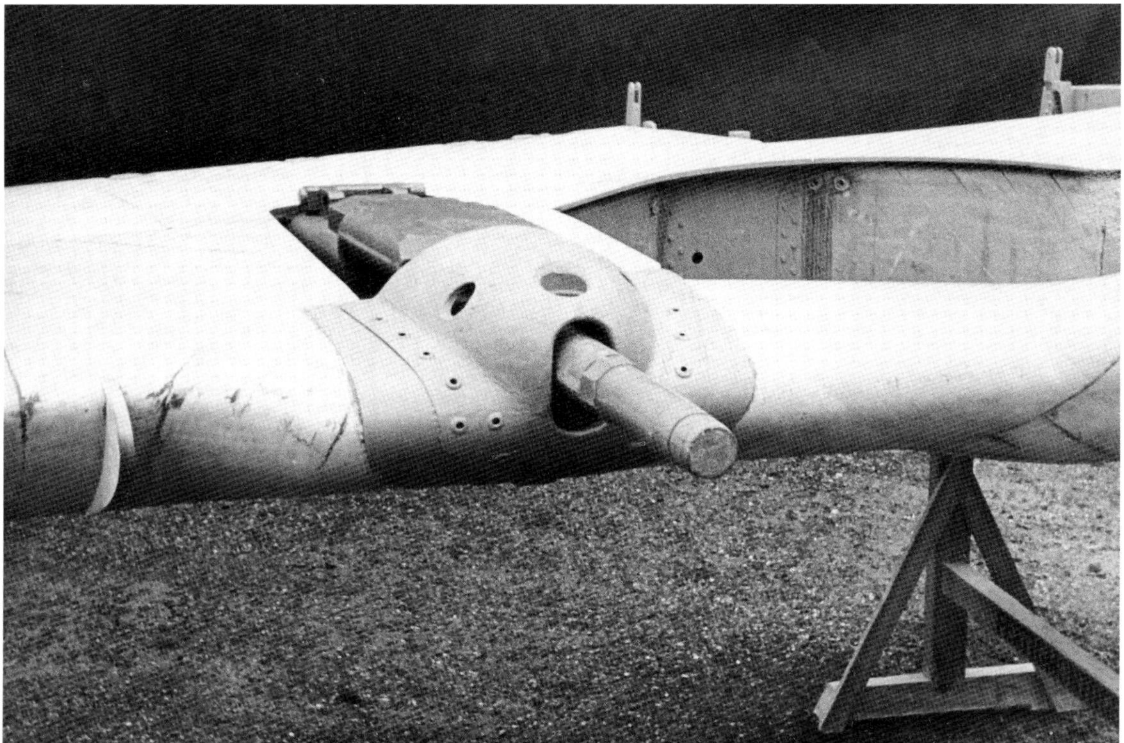

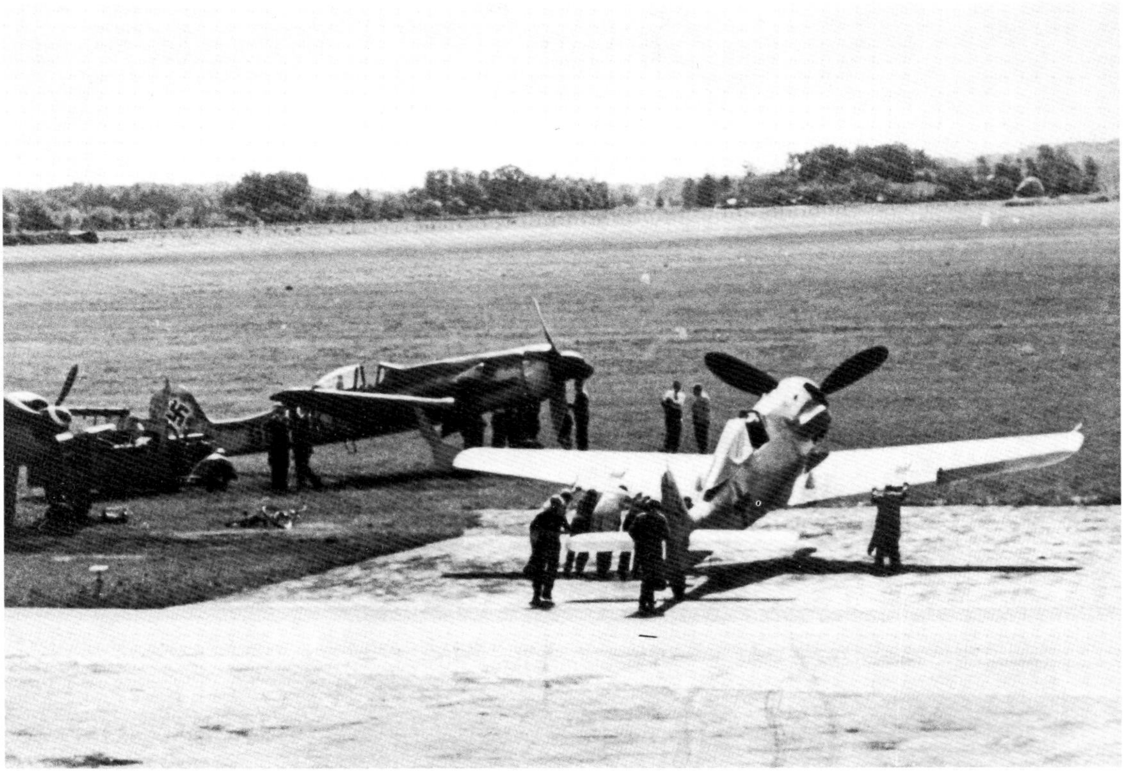

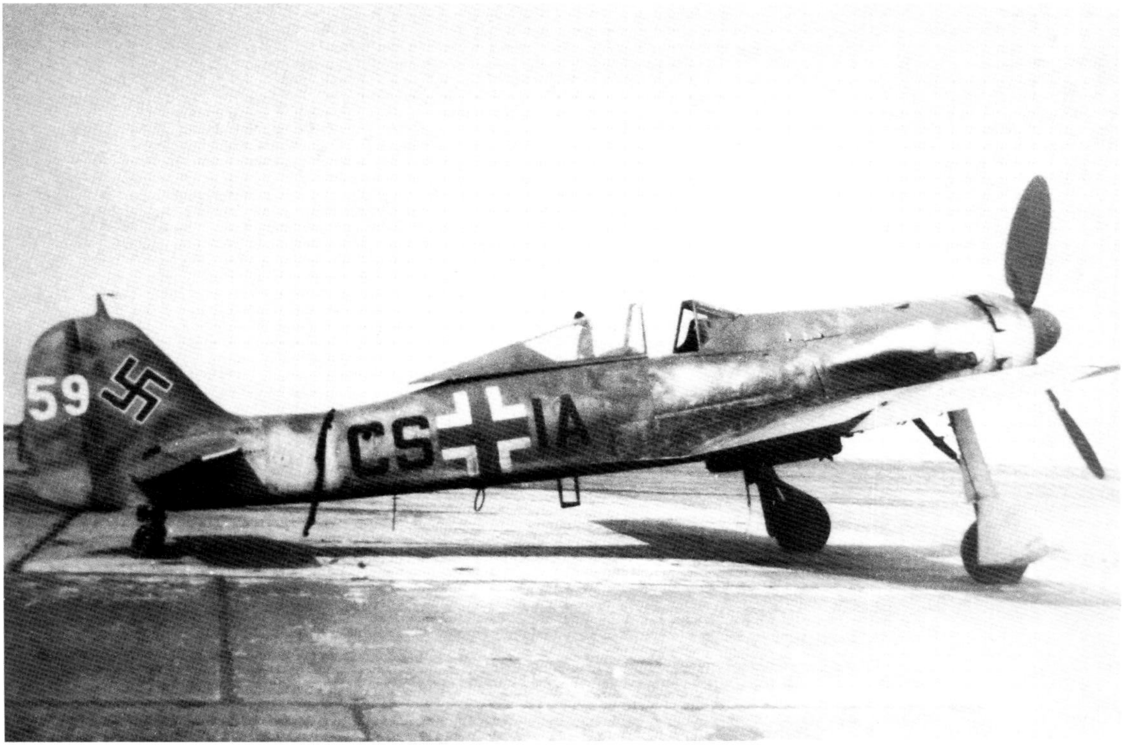
59
CS
IA

29•Above Left The Focke-Wulf airfield at Langenhagen near Hannover was just one of the places where aircraft producers tested their designs using their own airfields. The Langenhagen airfield was where the new Fw 190 D, the Ta 152 and the Ta 154 had all been evaluated in spite of several attacks by Allied fighters and bombers.

30•Below Left The Fw 190 V65, a prototype fitted with a Jumo 213 F engine, two MK 108 cannons and all-weather flying equipment, was used at Langenhagen until the end of 1944 and then transferred to *E-Stelle* Tarnewitz. It was there that the aircraft was captured together with a Ju 388 V6 just a few days before World War II ended in Europe.

31•Above Left The development of modern cockpit interiors became more and more important during the course of the war. The cockpit of the Fw 187 V1 prototype heavy fighter differed little from the pre-series aircraft completed later for further evaluation of the type. All necessary instrumentation was installed in the middle of the cockpit.

32•Above Right This view into the forward fuselage of the Me 264 V1 shows a prototype fitted only with those instruments necessary for the beginning of early flight tests. The second seat has been removed to gain a better view into the forward glazed section of the fuselage. The main flying instruments can be seen on a panel in the middle of the large console to the right of the pilot.

33•Right Several cabin mock-ups of the Ar 234 B had been constructed and built before the first prototype was rolled out. It perhaps shows how the interior of future combat aircraft would be laid out. The bomb sight on the Ar 234 was between the pilot's legs, with the console on the left containing the throttle quadrant for both port and starboard engines.

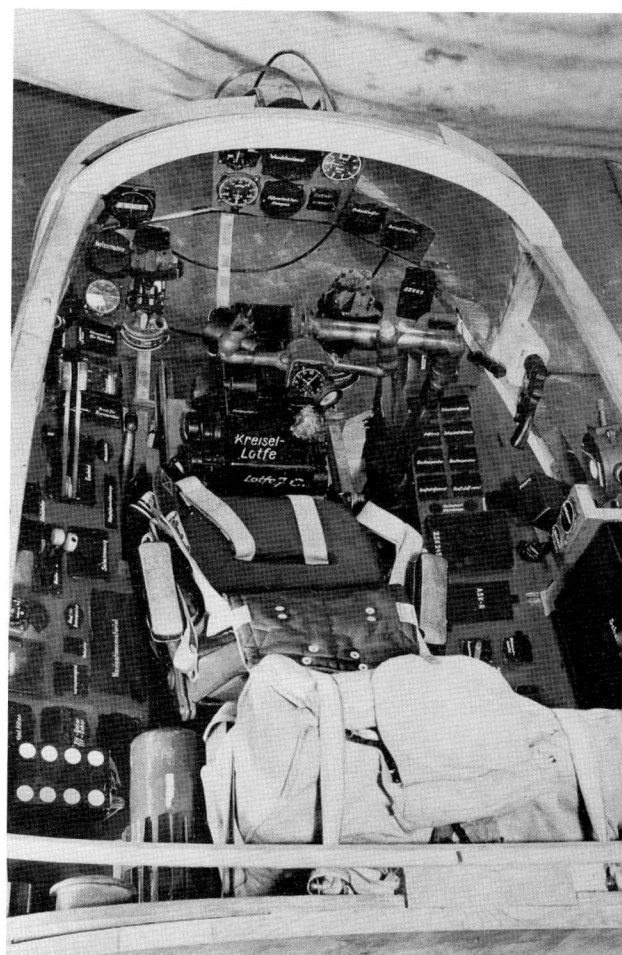

34•Above During the evaluation of the Fw 187 V1 (production number 949), it became obvious that the aircraft, powered by two Jumo 210 D engines, was 35 km/h faster than the Bf 109 single-engine fighter. However, since it was far easier and quicker to construct single-engine fighters, Focke-Wulf never received a large contract for the provision of the Fw 187.

35•Below The Bf 110 V3 prototype (D-ATII, production number 0870) was flown for the first time on 24 December 1936 powered by two DB 600 piston engines. In 1940, the aircraft was used for trials with more powerful DB 601s installed and the oil coolers suitably altered.

36•Above Right The Bf 162 V1 prototype (D-AABA, production number 811) was flown for the first time on 9 March 1938, with Dr. Herrmann Wurster at the controls. In 1939 the aircraft was handed over to the *E-Stelle* at Rechlin where it took part in a competition to find the fastest bomber of the time; its competitors were the Do 17, the Hs 127, the He 119 and the Ju 88.

37•Below Right As the German "Wooden Wonder", the Ta 154 (Ta was the assignation for aircraft designed by Kurt Tank) was estimated to be superior to allied combat aircraft in various respects. The RLM saw the 154's future role as a heavy aircraft destroyer, a night fighter and a light bomber. The Ta 154 V1 shown was flown at Langenhagen by Professor Tank himself.

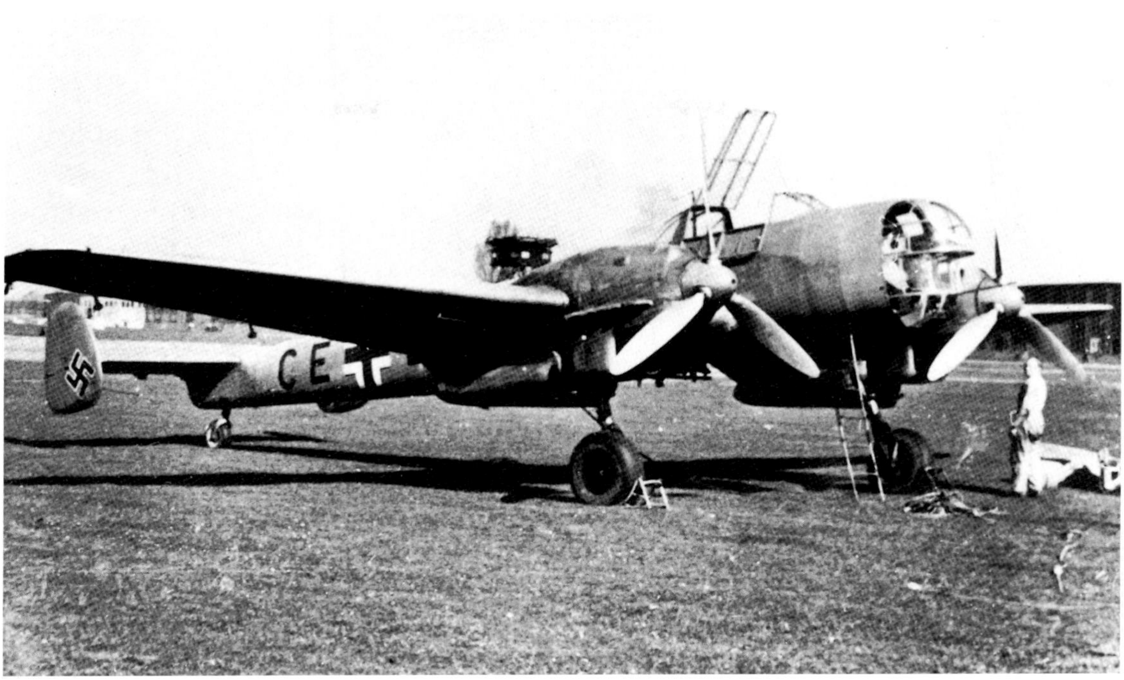
CE

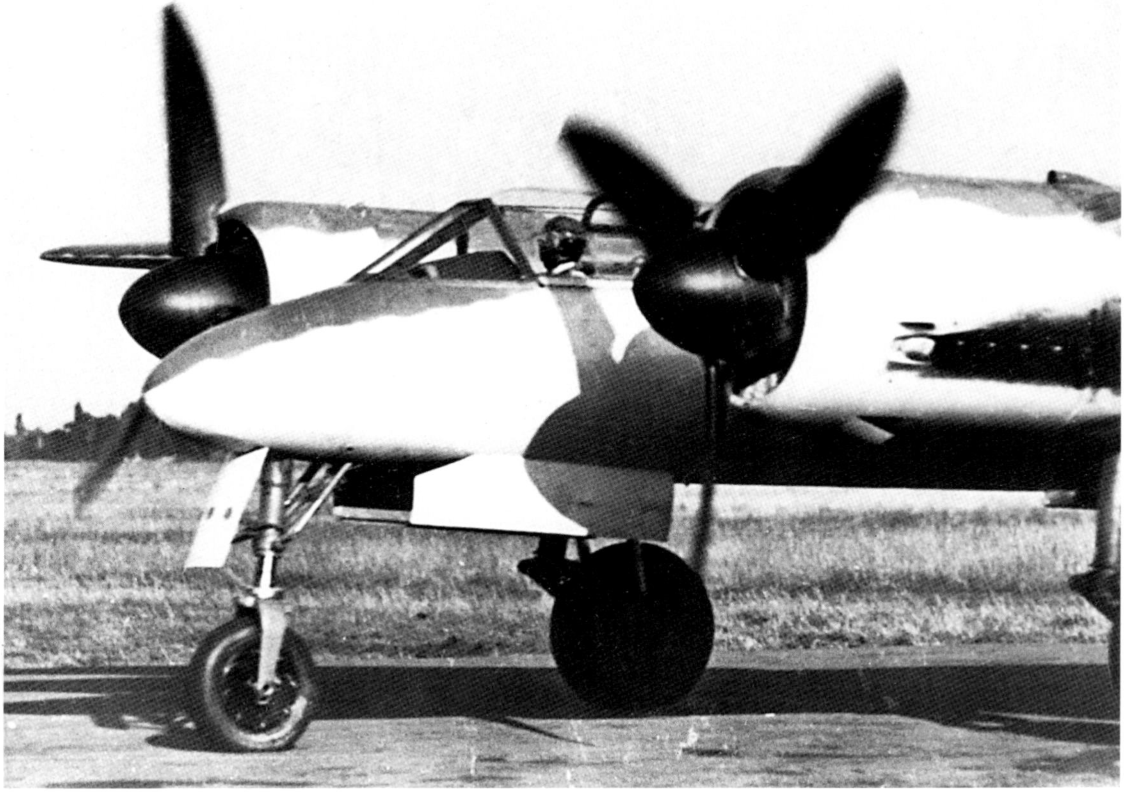

38 & 39 • Above and Below The Ar 240 belonged to a group of several aircraft which never quite made it, despite acceptable performance and an excellent equipment payload. Some prototypes and pre-series aircraft were handed over to the *Aufklärungsgruppe* (Reconnaissance Group) ObdL, where the Ar 240 A-04 proved itself fast enough to carry out reconnaissance missions over Great Britain until the middle of 1944. The aircraft subsequently crashed in Poland in the autumn of 1944 due to undercarriage failure.

40 • Above Several heavy destroyers were modified into night fighters, typically emerging from the many and varied Do 217s, Ju 88s and Bf 110s then available. The purpose-built He 219 *Uhu* (Owl) and the Ju 388 belonged to another small group of night fighters exhibiting high speed and powerful armament. The mock-up shown is a Ju 388 J night fighter with an early radar installation.

41 • Below This He 219 V33 (DV+DL, production number 190063) is an A-0 aircraft and was operated by the Telefunken works to evaluate the latest wireless sets then available (in the summer of 1944). The aircraft was proposed as a test bed for the new FuG 240 *Berlin* radar by *Erprobungsstellen* at Rechlin and Werneuchen.

42 • Above Parts of the He 219 V33 prototype, which was flown for the first time on 29 September 1943, were recovered from a lake in the middle of Germany on 6 October 2000. The aircraft can be seen standing near the runway at München-Riem in the summer of 1944.

43 • Below A few German single-engine fighters were completed as fast torpedo bombers. The aircraft shown (TD+SI, production number 871) was an experimental type used for the evaluation of the Fw 190 A-5/U15 series by the torpedo evaluation site at Gotenhafen-Hexengrund. The wing root housed two MG 151/20 guns.

44•Above Another shot of the same experimental aircraft, which could carry a standard Lt 5b aerial torpedo under an ETC 502 fitting under the main section of the fuselage. Besides testing the Fw 190 A as a fast torpedo bomber, other aircraft were used for tests with the BT 200, -400, -700 and -1400 under combat conditions during late summer 1944.

45•Below This Fw 190 A-8 was used as an experimental aircraft with a single BV 246 *Hagelkorn* missile fixed under an ETC 502 mounting. Only a few of these aircraft were built for drone tests in 1944, which were used in collaboration with He 111 H aircraft in evaluating the performance of this new air to ground weapon. Toward the end of the war, it was proposed filling the BV 246 with chemical warfare agents!

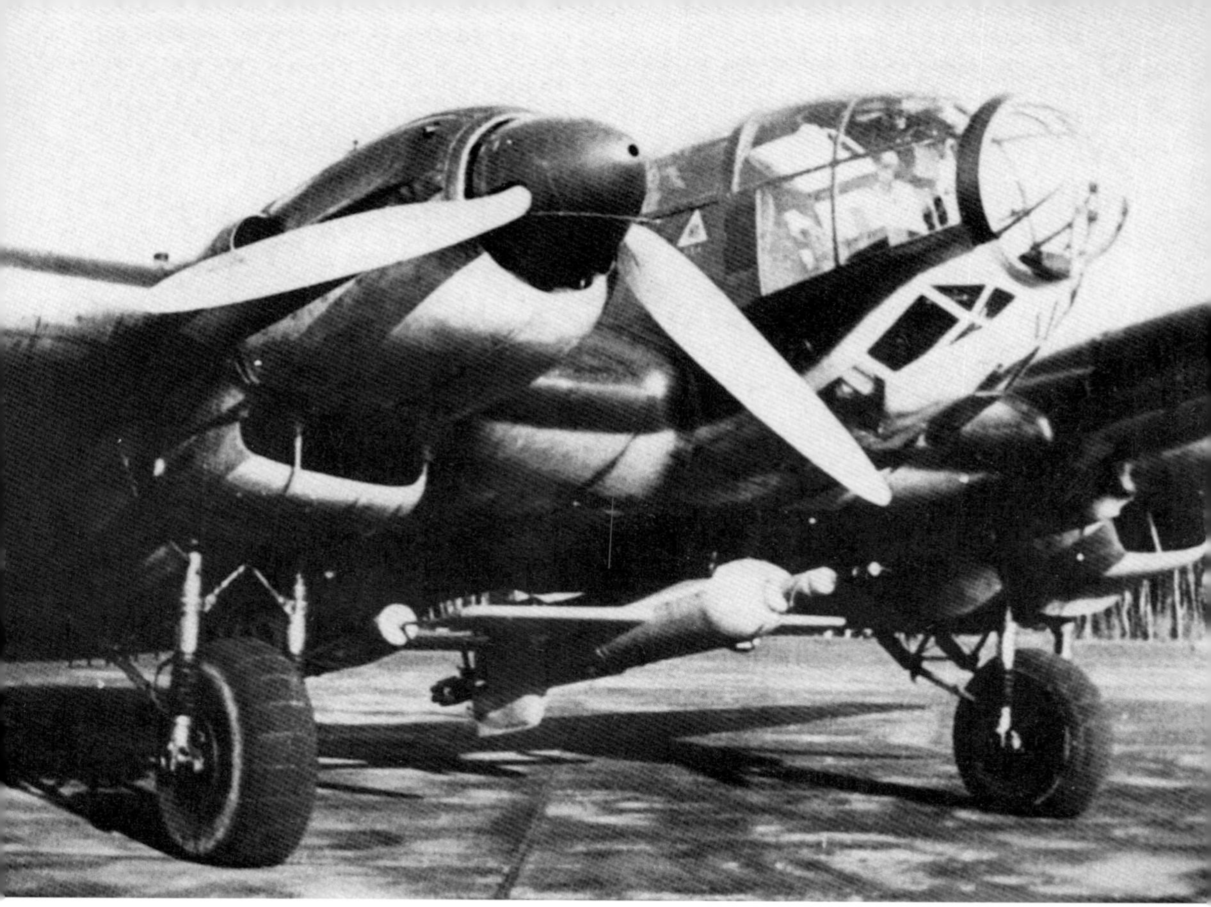

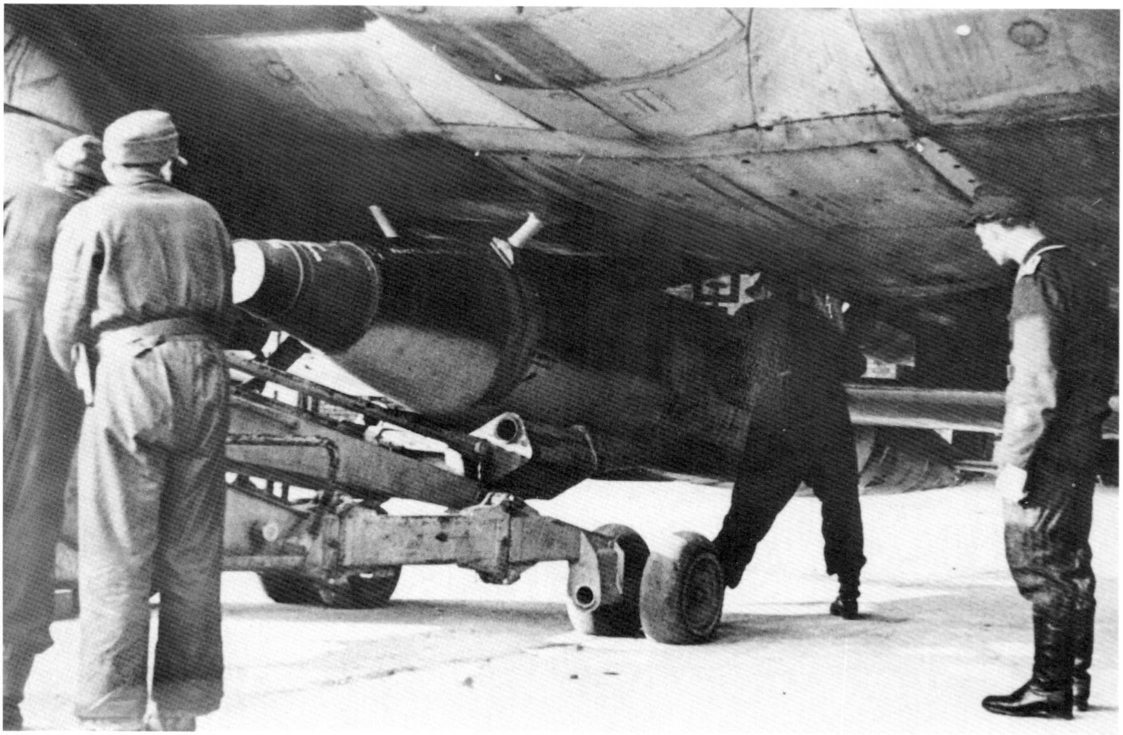

46•Above Left Several He 111 Hs were rebuilt to carry Henschel Hs 293 glide bombs. This early Hs 293 V2 was tested at the *E-Stelle* Peenemünde-West and was transported under the centreline of the aircraft. A decommissioned ship was used as the target vessel, moored not far from the Baltic coast.

47•Below Left After passing performance tests with a few modified He 111 H-16s in the middle of 1944, some 100 He 111 H-16 aircraft together with a few H-20 and H-22 variants were modified to carry FZG 76 V1 weapons. They were to be deployed over the North Sea heading for targets in England, since most of the land-based V1 installations had been hit by Allied bomber forces. When taking off, the V1's warhead was protected by a fairing (seen here) to prevent early detonation.

48•Above This He 111 H, seen at Peenemünde-West, was used for trials with the Lt 950 torpedo. The weapon shown was carried on a metal trolley and manouevred under the wing mount of the aircraft. At weapon-release, the torpedo fell from the mounting and commenced its (anticipated) journey toward the target. Despite many trials, the system never saw widespread deployment.

49•Below A few of the eight pre-series Ar 234 aircraft, including this one, S8 (GM+BH, production number 130008), were used for towing trials with a load-carrying air trailer. The trials were conducted at Neuburg near the Danube by the local *Versuchsgruppe* (Trials group) of the DFS. The first experimental trial was carried out by Erich Klöckner on 28 February 1945, but after the last test in the middle of March 1945, the trials were stopped.

50•Right Several He 111 Hs were used for testing new equipment for future Luftwaffe combat aircraft. Much new special equipment needed to be installed, especially for the evaluation of more powerful torpedo bombers. The photo shows a Lichtenstein BC/T (FuG 202 T) device, used for anti-shipping raids, which was tested at Gotenhafen-Hexengrund.

51•Below The testing and evaluation of the remote-controlled FDL 131/C gun turret, as fitted on both sides of the fuselage of the Me 410 combat aircraft seen here, was a very lengthy process due to numerous technical problems arising when operating the weapons in flight. The work on the system was carried out under the auspices of the KdE.

52•Far Right Above This Ju 88 C-6, based at Werneuchen, was fitted with a turnable turret housing two 3 cm MK 103 guns, each of which was fitted with 200 explosive rounds of varying kinds. The weapons were remotely operated by a Telefunken FuG 212 system or similar fitted in the fuselage. Since the turret was viewed as largely responsible for reducing the aircraft's speed, all plans for its deployment were cancelled.

53•Far Right Below The He 177 A-1 was modified to be evaluated under combat conditions with a double moveable weapon mount fitted in the nose. The first prototype, the He 177 V12 (GI+BL), was tested at Tarnewitz with two MK 101 cannons but with only limited success.

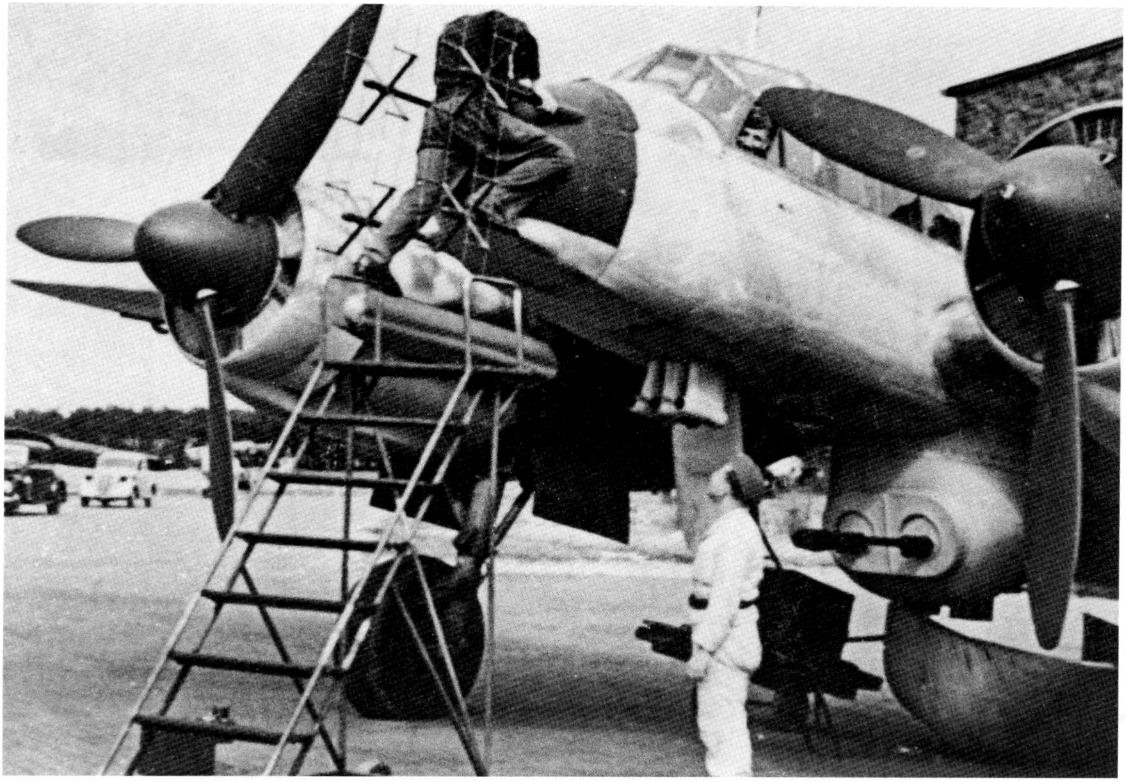

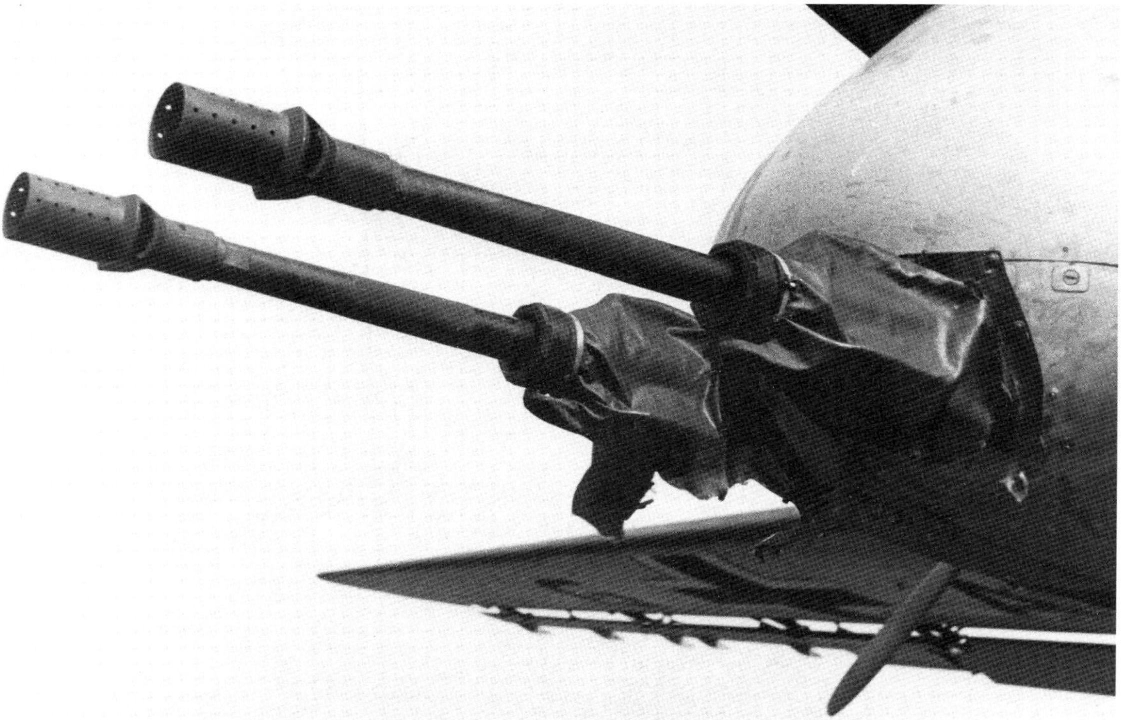

54•Above This photo was taken in December 1932 at Travemünde, during tests carried out on the He 60b (D-2325), which was powered by a BMW VIu piston engine. Test pilots and technicians pose in front of the aircraft to take a memorable photo of RDL personnel.

55•A He 59 crew greet their comrades on their way back from their designated test sector over the Baltic during RDL torpedo evaluation trials at Travemünde. Note that it was unusual to fit any armaments during evaluation trials.

56•Several high ranking officers of the German Wehrmacht were sent to Travemünde and other Luftwaffe evaluation sites to familiarise themselves with (then) new technology. This He 60 short-range reconnaissance aircraft sits atop a catapult used on larger warships of the Kriegsmarine in readiness for launching.

57•The first prototype of the Hamburger Flugzeugbau Ha 138 long-range reconnaissance flying boat (later the BV 138 V2, D-AMOR, production number 113) was first flown on 14 July 1936. The flying boat differed from the V1 prototype (production number 114) in having a new wing layout. The defensive armament positions would subsequently be altered.

58•Left The Blohm & Voss BV 222 was amongst the largest of the flying boats operated by the Luftwaffe after the outbreak of World War II. Deutsche Lufthansa was not allowed to take the first prototype *Wiking* (Viking), so rather than being an aircraft on, say, long-range postal service work, the BV 222 was evaluated as a long-range transport for the Luftwaffe, capable as it was of carrying large loads such as aircraft engines or similar.

59 & 60•Right The Göppingen Gö 9 was built as a flying scale-model of the Dornier project P 192, which later became the huge Do 214 flying boat. The smaller model was constructed in wood and was, of course, far cheaper than a full size flying boat whilst achieving the same results during flying tests. The project was undertaken by the technical high school at Göppingen and built by the Hirth Works. Both pictures show preparations for the transport of the scale-model.

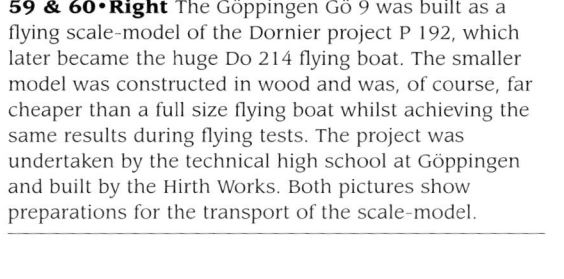

61•Below The largest German flying boat ever was constructed and manufactured by Blohm & Voss at Hamburg-Finkenwerder near the Elbe River. Despite its huge size, the BV 238 V1 took off for the first time, with no problems, on 10 March 1944. Due to its dimensions, the one and only BV 238 prototype was never tested by the *Erprobungsstelle* Travemünde but hidden on the shores of the Schaalsee.

62•Above Left The first Fi 156 (D-IBXY) was much different to the later pre-series and series aircraft. During its evaluation it became obvious that its flight characteristics could be achieved by a fuselage and fin section of simpler construction and wings of a simpler geometry. This aircraft was later rebuilt to these new standards and received the aircraft callsign PO+AL.

63•Below Left Although the Fi 156 demonstrated superb performance in daily service, the Luftwaffe wanted an enlarged four-seat version of all-metal construction and exhibiting even better performance. The Fi 256 V1 was flown for the first time on 9 July 1941 with Dipl.-Ing. Willy Fiedler at the controls.

64•Below During the early years of World War II, the majority of the Luftwaffe's air transport capacity depended on the Ju 52/3m. However, despite its strength, this transport ideally needed a prepared runway when taking off. Because of this shortcomng, Arado proposed its Ar 232 as the Luftwaffe's first truly all-terrain transport. The picture show the first prototype, Ar 232 V1 (GH+GN).

65•Above Right Another transport design was evaluated along with the Ju 52/3m and the Ar 232/432 during the war. The picture shows the second Ju 352 V1 (CH+JA, production number 100001) at Fritzlar during maintenance work. The first Ju 352 tested was the former Ju 252 V1/1 (BH+DB) which was flown as Ju 352 V0 on 18 March 1943.

66•Below Right The Fw 200 V1 in this picture is seen warming up its Pratt & Whitney Hornet radials before its first take-off from the Neuenlander Feld on 6 September 1937. The aircraft was intensively tested as D-AERE and was refitted with BMW 132 L radials. Subsequently the aircraft received the callsign D-ACON and carried out its famous non-stop flight from Berlin to New York.

67 • Above The DFS 230 was introduced as a so-called *Lastensegler* (shortened to LS 1 and which means cargo glider) by the *Deutsche Forschungsanstalt für Segelflug* (German gliding investigation organisation, or DFS). The development was started in mid-1936, the first three experimental gliders being designated as *Studien Versuchsflugzeuge* (study experimentals) and which were tested by the DFS and the Luftwaffe at Stendal until March 1937.

68 • Below To train new pilots to fly the German *Gigant* aircraft, especially the huge Me 321 gliders, a DFS 230 was placed on a wheeled undercarriage to give the pilot the impression of sitting in a much larger glider. It is still unknown whether more than just the one aircraft shown (CB+MW) was built.

69•Above Another experimental version of the DFS 230 was tested as a sea-glider and was fitted with two floats taken from an Ar 196 float plane. It is possible that the trials were carried out to evaluate a transport glider suitable for special operations by the *Brandenburger*, the legendary German commando unit. With the exception of a very small cross on the side of the fuselage, there are no further national emblems visible.

70•Below This version of a modified Go 242 glider was tested by the Luftwaffe. Unlike the series-produced Go 242 and Go 244, the double fin section was changed into a central fin section. It is possible that this evaluation project was carried out to collect reliable data relating to the Kalkert Ka 430 glider, first drawings of which were made early in 1944 by *Reparaturwerk Erfurt GmbH*.

71•Above Left To move a huge Me 321 glider it became necessary to use aircraft with enough power as towing aircraft: either a four-engined Ju 290, a five-engined He 111 Z or three Bf 110s. The trials illustrated shows the Ju 290 Z-3 (KB+LA, production number 90 0002), with many *Giganten* (Giants) dispersed aound the airfield awaiting a first test flight.

72•Middle Left Less than twenty He 111 Z-1s were produced for the towing of large transport gliders. Many dangers presented themselves during their evaluation caused by the excessive take-off weight of the heavily-laden Me 321s. Only with all five engines running would enough tractive effort be available to effect a safe take-off. Several tests with alternative glider loadings were undertaken to gather reliable data for frontline service.

73•Below Left The initial tests of the largest German glider, the Ju 322 V1 *Mammut* (Mammoth), failed. The huge glider was developed as the Junkers EF 94 and exhibited a wing span of 64.8 m. During the first attempt to lift the giant off the ground, the prototype demonstrated great instability and flew only a short distance after the pilot of the towing Ju 90 Z-3 released the towing cable in an emergency. The project was subsequently cancelled.

74•Below Much work was done to develop a small but very effective helicopter for liaison and reconnaissance duties, to be used by the Kriegsmarine, the Luftwaffe and the German Army. The Flettner Fl 282 V6 shown (GF+YF) was tested on board the minelayer *Drache* (Dragon) in the Mediterranean Sea, with great success. Later, 3./*Bordfliegergruppe* 196 received Fa 230 and Fl 282 helicopters for special use on board ships and submarines of the Kriegsmarine.

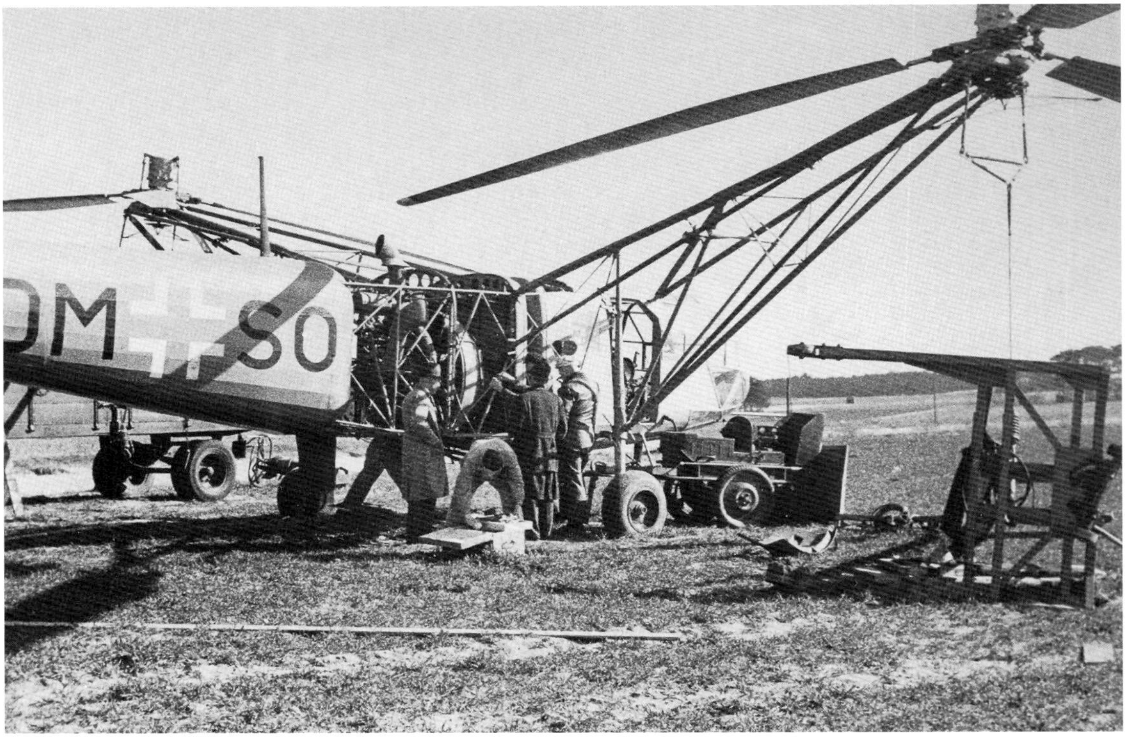
DM
SO

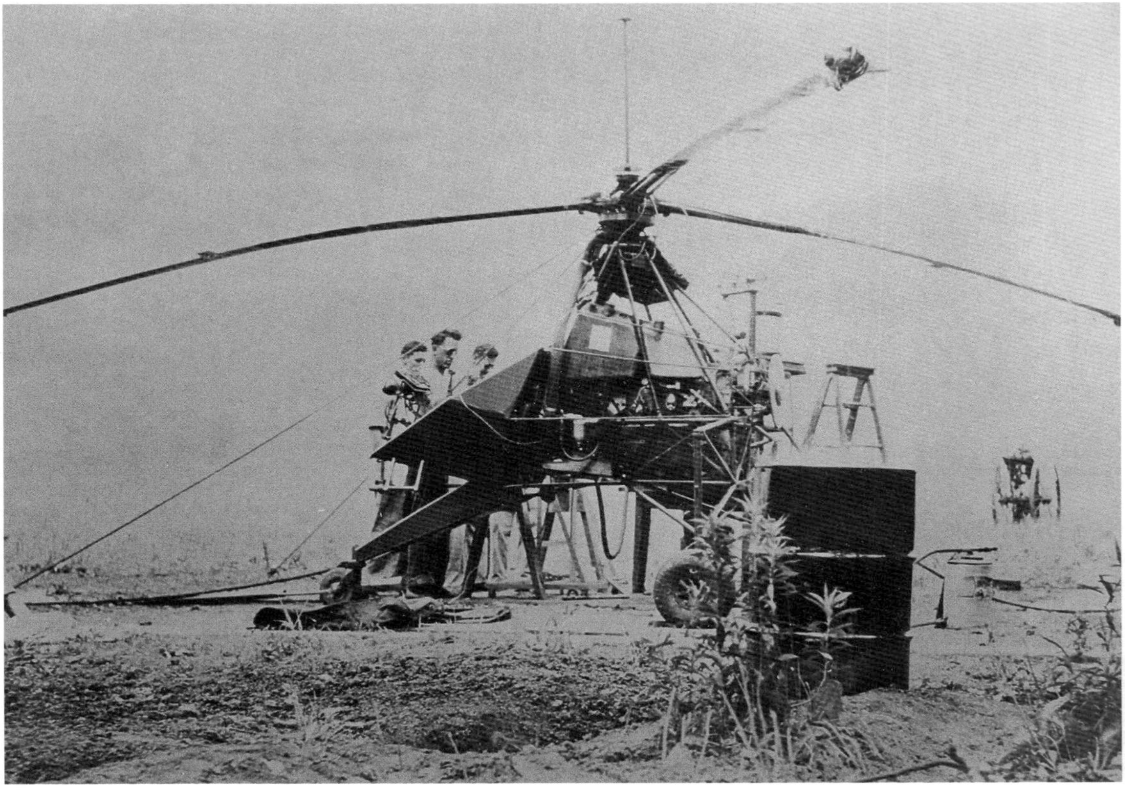

75 • Above Left After building just three Fa 223s (V1 to V3), the following seven partly-completed aircraft were lost when Allied bombs hit Hoyenkampf near Delmenhorst on 4 June 1942. The next experimental version was the Fa 223 V11 (DM+SO, production number 00011) the engine of which failed during an evaluation near Münster / Westfalen. Despite the conditions, it was quite feasible to install a new BMW 301 Q3 Fafnir in the field!

76 • Below Left Four WNF 342 helicopters were designed and later constructed from an idea of Dipl.-Ing. Friedrich von Doblhoff. The first one was tested in September 1943 in a large hangar. After its initial tests, the WNF 342 V4 experimetal helicopter was captured at Obergrafendorf by American ground forces early in 1945.

77 • Above The Junkers EF 61 was an experimental type only used in researching high-altitude flight. Only two of these aircraft were manufactured of which the first one, the EF 61 E1 (production number 4931) first flew on 4 March 1937, crashing six months later on 10 September 1937. The second of the two entered flight testing on 18 December 1937.

78 • Below In addition to the Junkers EF 61, the Henschel works at Schönefeld near Berlin built another experimental aircraft for high-altitude flight research. It was hoped, of course, to lead to the development of aircraft which would operate at altitudes where no enemy fighter or anti-aircraft guns could oppose them. The aircraft shown was the second Hs 128 V2 (D-ARHD), which was flown for the first time in March 1940.

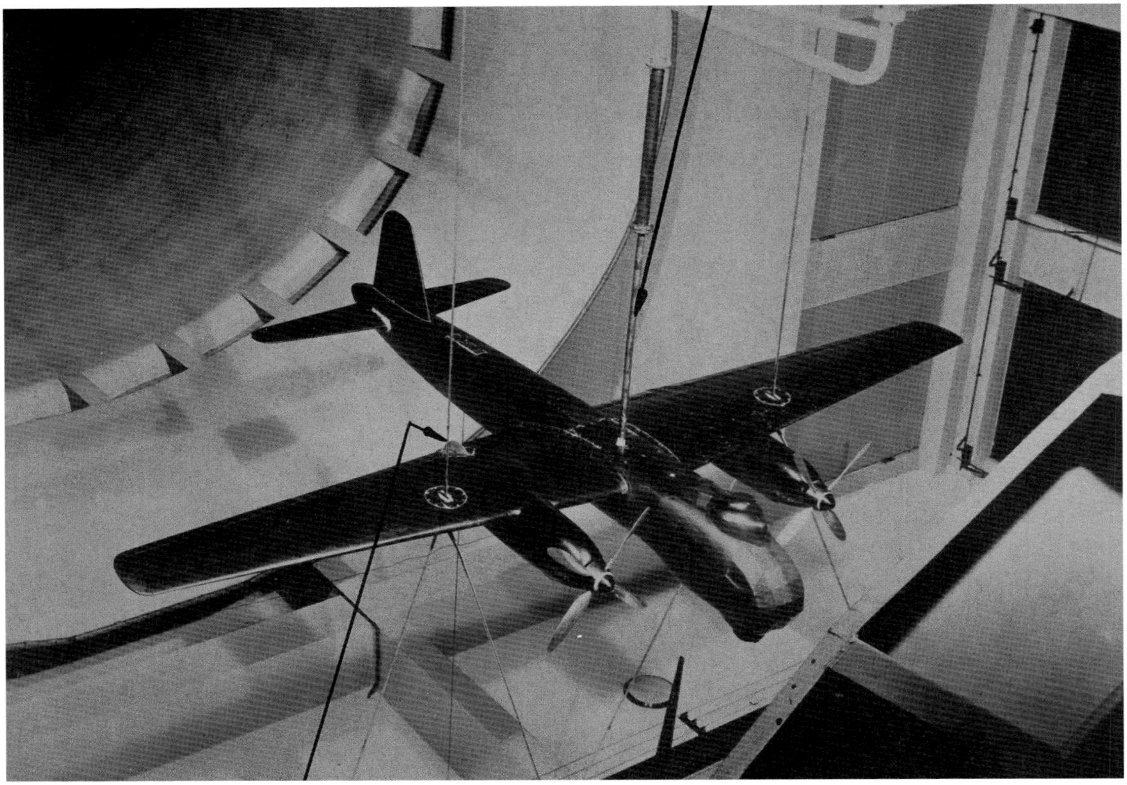

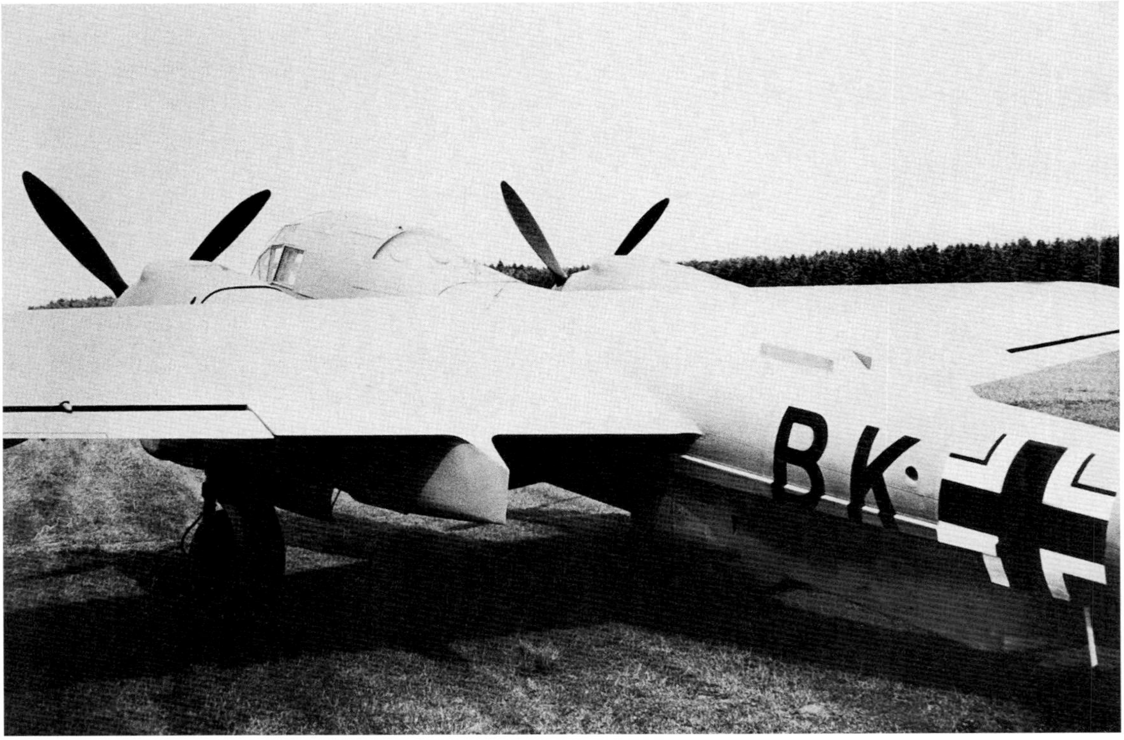
BK

79•Above Left Following flight tests of the Hs 130 A-0 reconnaissance aircraft, a second version, to be used as a bomber and designated the B-0, was designed but never built. Instead, the Hs 130 C-0 was proposed, a wooden mock-up of which was intensively tested in the wind tunnel of the AVA at Göttingen. However, only three prototypes had left the Henschel works by June 1942.

80•Below Left Dornier also put forward its own designs for a high-altitude combat aircraft, proposing the use of two special piston engines. The first prototype, the Do 217 PV1 (BK+IR, production number 1229) first flew on 3 August 1942. Three evaluation aircraft were completed but two more were scrapped before their final assembly.

81•Above Right Besides the Ju 86 P/R, the Hs 130 A/C/E and the Do 217 P, a number of additional designs for a high-altitude reconnaissance aircraft were proposed by the DFS during World War II. After the construction of one of their gliders was stopped by the RLM, the DFS signed a contract to build two rocket-powered gliders which could reach an altitude of some 20,000 metres. The aircraft were transported by the third pre-series Do 217 K-3.

82•Below Right Only two aircraft of the DFS 228 type were completed. The first one (V1, D-IBFQ) was tested during October 1944. The second aircraft joined the flight test program on 21 December 1944 but was destroyed during an Allied air raid at Rechlin a short time later. The DFS 228 V1 was captured by US ground forces early in 1945 at the Luftwaffe base at Hörsching. Dipl.Ing. Ziegler can be seen standing in the cockpit of the V1 prototype.

83•Below Many experimental aircraft were needed to carry out all kinds of engine development. In addition, engineers and technicians set about finding new ways to fit powerplants to gliders. The DFS 230 shown was fitted with two Argus ramjets by the DFS at Ainring near Bad Reichenhall in Bavaria. The tests were observed by the Officer Commanding, *Generalfeldmarschall* Milch.

84•Above To evaluate the performance of the different series of the Argus 014 ramjet, a two-seat light aircraft was used with one of these engines fitted beneath its fuselage. The Go 145 (D-IIWS) shown was operated from 30 April 1941 from Berlin-Schönefeld. The photo was taken by the crew of a He 46 which accompanied the experimental aircraft during its test program.

85•Below From 16 September 1943 to 30 August 1944, Erich Klöckner made a number of test flights in the Do 217 E-2 (RE+CD), which had been fitted with a 10.6 metre-long, 1.5 metre diameter, high-temperature ramjet fitted on the fuselage. The first trials, with a smaller Pulso-Rohr ramjet, had already taken place on 7 March 1942 using a Do 17 experimental aircraft. The large ramjet developed 20,000 hp and boosted the Do 217's speed to 700 km/h.

86•Above Unknown problems with the Daimler-Benz engines, with their fairings too close to the He 177 aircraft's skin, were responsible for several losses during the flight evaluation program of this four-piston-engined German bomber. The first prototype, He 177 V2 (CB+RQ, production number 0002), was mainly used for stability tests and the evaluation of a new horizontal tailplane.

87•Below The He 177 V29 (GO+IF, production number 15155), an aircraft belonging to the A-1 series, was mainly used for defensive armament trials at the *E-Stelle* Rechlin. Note a small remote-controlled weapons turret could be installed in the lower front section of the aircraft.

88•Above The eleventh prototype of the Ju 288 (V11, D-ANXN, later DF+CQ, production number 0011) took off for the first time on 21 July 1942, after the aircraft had received new DB 606 engines in May 1942. Despite many subsequent alterations, the Ju 288 was never introduced by the Luftwaffe, production being ceased after only a few Ju 288s belonging to the first pre-series (C-0) had been manufactured.

89•Below A quite similar fate as befell the Ju 288 was suffered by the Me 264, only one experimental aircraft ever being completed. A second aircraft was destroyed during an Allied bombing raid while the parts for all other prototypes were scrapped after the project was cancelled due to the course of the war. RE+EN was itself subsequently destroyed during a bombing raid on 18 July 1944.

90•Above Right Of the four He 177 B-5 long-range prototypes ordered by the RLM, none ever became available for the Luftwaffe. V101 (NN+QQ), pictured here, an A-3 rebuilt to B-5 standards, was the first of the four. In August 1944, the new prototype, with four single engines fitted, joined the flight development program.

91•Below Right Only two prototypes of the Ju 287 were built. The first (RS+RA) was flown for the first time on 8 August 1944. The fuselage was rebuilt from a He 177 A-3 while the rear and the fin section were taken from a Ju 188 G-2 experimental aircraft. Besides the fixed main landing gear, the forward undercarriage was taken from a captured B-24 bomber!

92•Above Left As Allied air raids increasingly devastated more of the Germans' infrastructure, the RLM looked for small aircraft, so-called point-defence fighters, which could be produced easily in smaller factories, the most numerous being the Me 163. Only some 70 B-series experimental aircraft were built, and these were handed over to *Erprobungskommando* (EK) 16, as well as to other evaluation units of the Luftwaffe.

93 & 94•Middle Left & Below Left The prototypes of the Me 328 were experimental aircraft built by Messerschmitt/DFS and the Jacobs-Schweyer aircraft factories. A small initial batch was ordered by the RLM, consisting of ten A-series experimental aircraft, the Me 328 V1 to V10, followed by a further 20 experimental aircraft which were the forerunners of the final Me 328 B design. The aircraft shown, without its final paint finish, could have been the second prototype for the A series. Flight tests were carried out by the DFS at Ainring in Bavaria.

95•Above On 16 July 1942, Fritz Wendel took off in the third prototype of the Me 262 (PC+UC), seen standing under the huge wings of a Me 321 transport glider at Leipheim near Ulm/Donau. The aircraft was powered by two early Jumo 004 jet engines fitted beneath the wings. An artificer from Junkers Motorenwerke (Jumo) can be seen working on the port engine.

97•Below The development of many German jet-powered combat aircraft was never completed due to a shortage of jet engines, missing parts or other problems arising from Allied bombing raids. One such was the Focke-Wulf "*TL-Jäger mit HeS 011*" (Jet fighter with a single Heinkel HeS 011 jet engine). Many variants of it were proposed but never realised.

98•Above Right The first and second Bachem BP 20 *Natter* (Adder), designated M1 and M2, were tested by both Bachem and the DFS at the Luftwaffe airfield at Neuburg/Donau. The first manned experiment was carried out on 3 November 1944, but after releasing the M1 from a towing He 111 of the DFS, the aircraft crashed and was totally destroyed. The first manned vertical take-off of the *Natter* occurred on 1 March 1945.

96•Above Because of the new but unfamiliar engines chosen for the Me 262 jet fighter, several experimental aircraft were needed to speed up the evaluation program of the type. Most of the early series aircraft were handed over to the *Erprobungskommando* 262, which was based at Lechfeld near Augsburg as of early July 1944. *Kommando Nowotny*, comprising a staff and three *Staffeln*, were also used for subsequent tactical evaluation.

99•Below Right The second prototype of the Horten H IX V2, which was equipped with two Jumo 004 Bs, was flown by Erwin Ziller on 18 December 1944. The first official take off occurred on 2 February 1945, but after one of the engines failed during one of the following tests, the flying wing hit the ground with one wing tip and crashed. Erwin Ziller was killed in the accident.

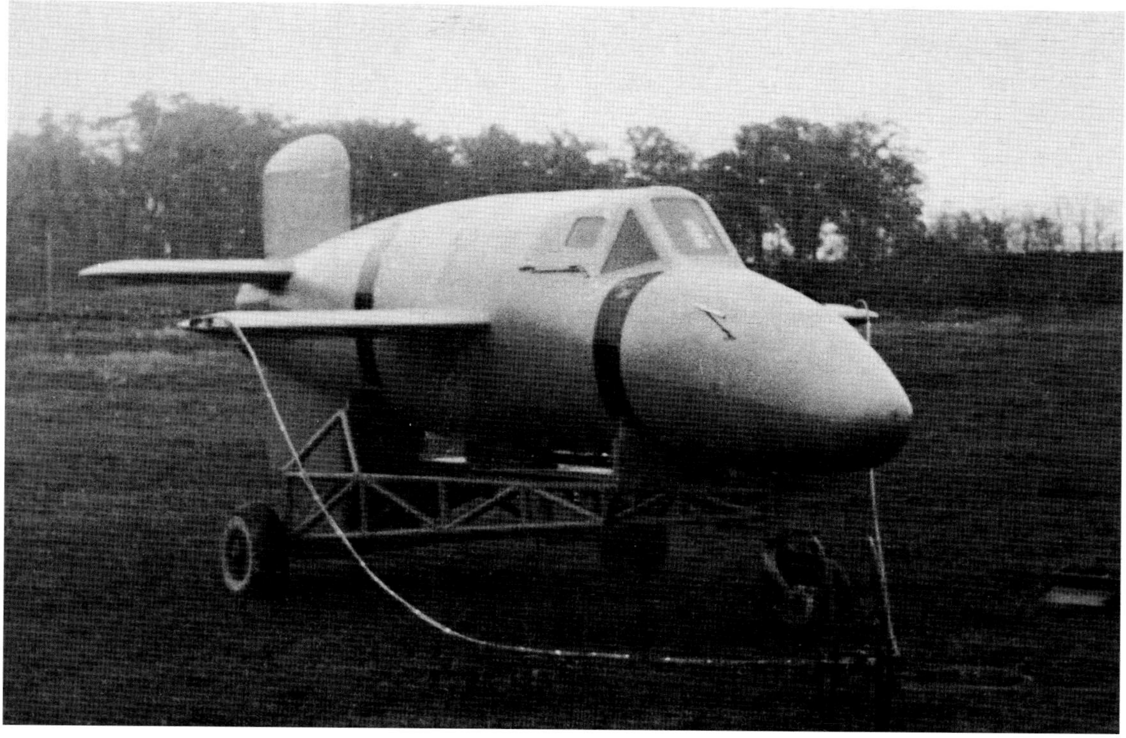

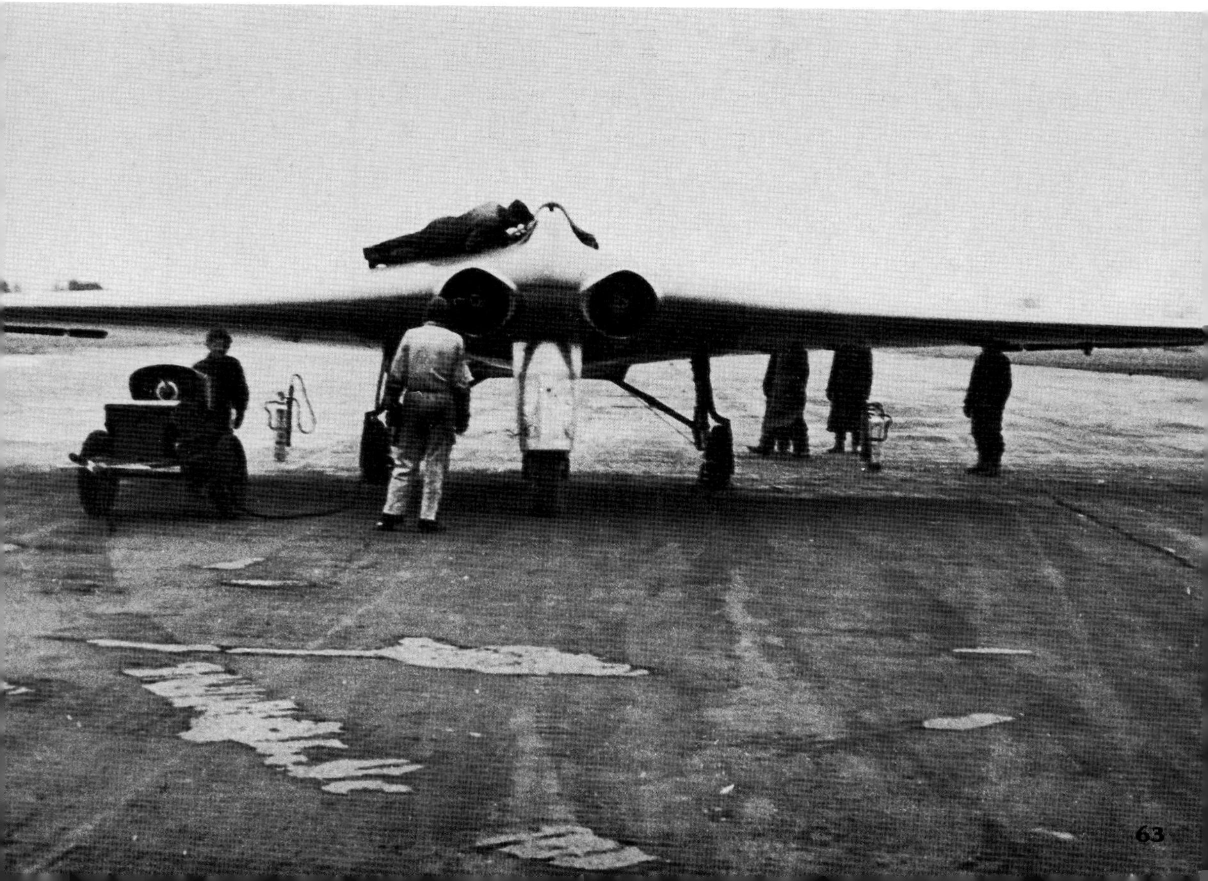

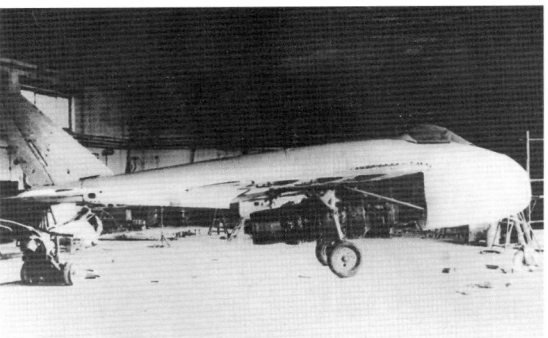

100•Above The Messerschmitt P 1101 was a German research aircraft with a single engine fitted in the fuselage and demonstrating swept-back wings. When American soldiers entered Oberammergau in Bavaria, the design was about 80% complete, but due to the general lack of HeS 011 turbojet engines there had been no chance to finish the work any earlier on the prototype.

101•Left This picture of a Bachem *Natter* was taken in southern Germany in 1944/45. It shows the huge Wehrmacht exercise ground at Heuberg near Stetten am Kalten Markt, where different launch platforms for the Ba 349 *Natter* had been installed.

102•Above Right The Göppingen Gö 9 (D-EBYW) was used for testing the Do 335 aircraft. The Gö 9 featured a model Do 17 fuselage and wings in 1/2.5 scale and was fitted with a small Hirth HM 60 R engine of 80 hp. This experimental aircraft took off for the first time in early 1940 from Mengen/Württemberg and was later flown from Wüsterberg, where this photo was taken in the same year.

103•Below Right Between 1935 and 1940, several He 70s were used for testing new equipment by the *Kommando der Erprobungsstellen* situated at the *Erprobungsstelle* Rechlin near Lake Müritz, east of Berlin, and at other evaluation sites too. Unarmed He 70s were used for personnel transport or liaison duties until the early forties.

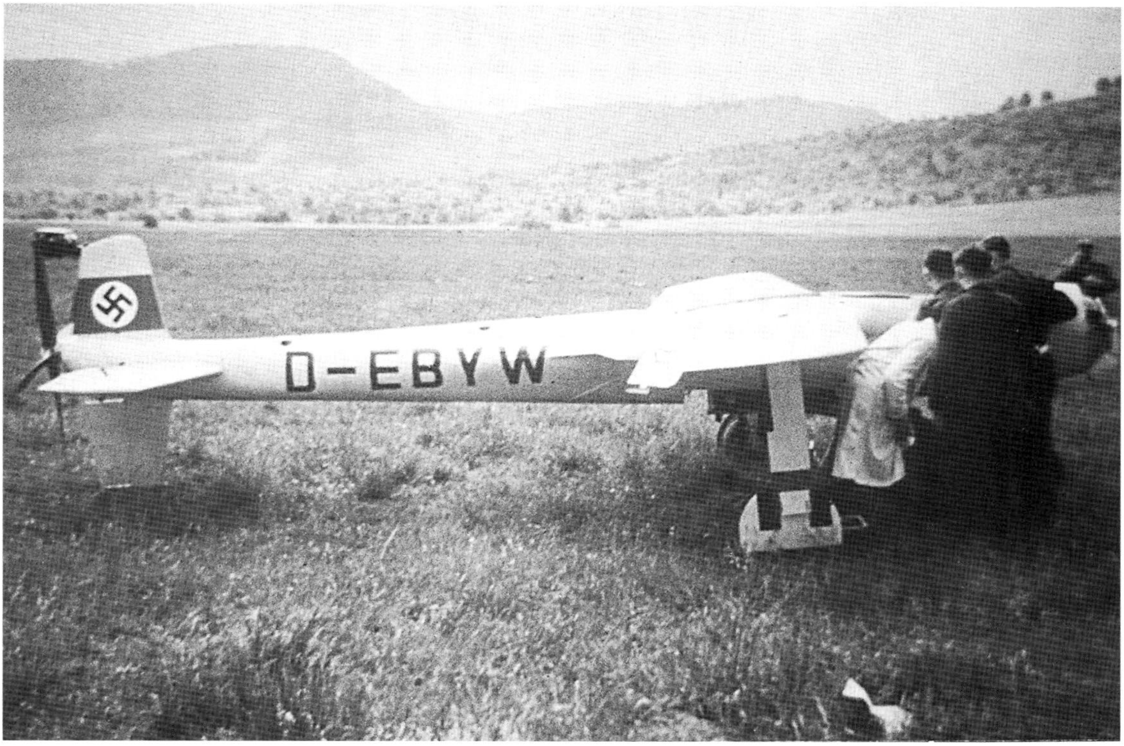
D-EBYW

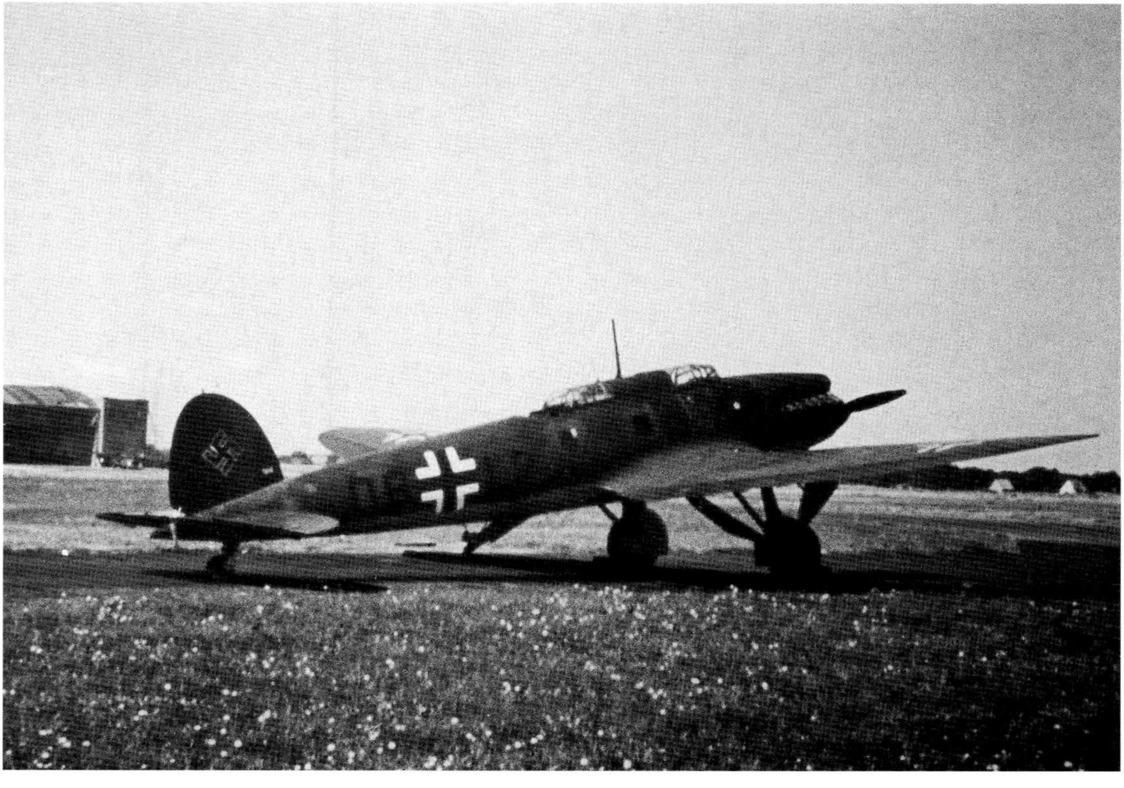

104•Above There were three experimental versions of the Heinkel He 116, of which the first entered flight development on 9 December 1936, some twelve series aircraft having been manufactured. One was lost, however, flying for the *Versuchsstelle für Höhenflüge* on 16 January 1941. The aircraft shown stands before a hangar at Zwischenahn near Oldenburg and belonged to *Luftdienstkommando* 61.

105•below By 7 May 1940, the *Erprobungsstelle der Luftwaffe* at Travemünde operated ten He 115s for evaluation duties. With the exception of He 115s V2 to V5, four A-0s and a single B-aircraft, equipped with an enlarged bomb release system, were tested. The aircraft shown has just been tested by a crew based at the Heinkel works at nearby Warnemünde.

106•Above The first stage of testing the Do 26 was conducted at the Dornier works at Friedrichshafen on the shores of Lake Constance. Later, the aircraft was handed over to the Luftwaffe for further evaluation. Despite the Lufthansa insignia, the Do 26s never were the property of the well-known carrier. All six Do 26s were subsequently handed over to the Luftwaffe complete with crews formerly employed by Lufthansa.

107•Below The Ju 388 L-1 was one of the last Luftwaffe combat aircraft powered by piston engines capable of high-altitude flying. Those few aircraft handed over to the Luftwaffe frontline units were well equipped with modern electronics systems, then becoming available (in late 1944). This included rear warning systems and many new types of wireless set.

108•Above Only a limited number of Ju 290 A long-range reconnaissance aircraft were tested at Rechlin. Most Ju 90s and Ju 290s sent to Rechlin were destined to be out-and-out combat aircraft or long-range transports. This maritime reconnaissance aircraft has been fitted with a FuG 200 radar and heavy defensive armament.

110•Above Right After the loss of the seventh experimental Me 262 (production number 130007), another Me 262 A-1, which was flown from October 1944, became the new seventh prototype, and was designated V 303 (production number 170 303). The aircraft was used for the development of a high-speed jet bomber capable of transporting two 250 kg GP bombs or other weapons under ETC mountings fixed beneath the forward fuselage.

111•Below Right This Me 262 A-1a's number, V056, was derived from its production number 170056. The aircraft was used for the testing of radar antennas under high speed conditions. This experimental aircraft was the first jet-powered type specifically used to support the development of the high-speed night fighter variant, the Me 262 B-2. With the exception of a small batch of Me 262 B-1a/U1 auxiliary night fighters, it is highly probable that no more were manufactured.

109•Above During its early development, the third experimental Me 262 aircraft was the first to be flown powered by two early Jumo jet engines. This photo was taken on the runway of the Luftwaffe air base at Leipheim during final work on the starboard Jumo T1. The first flight occurred on 18 July 1942 with Fritz Wendel at the controls.

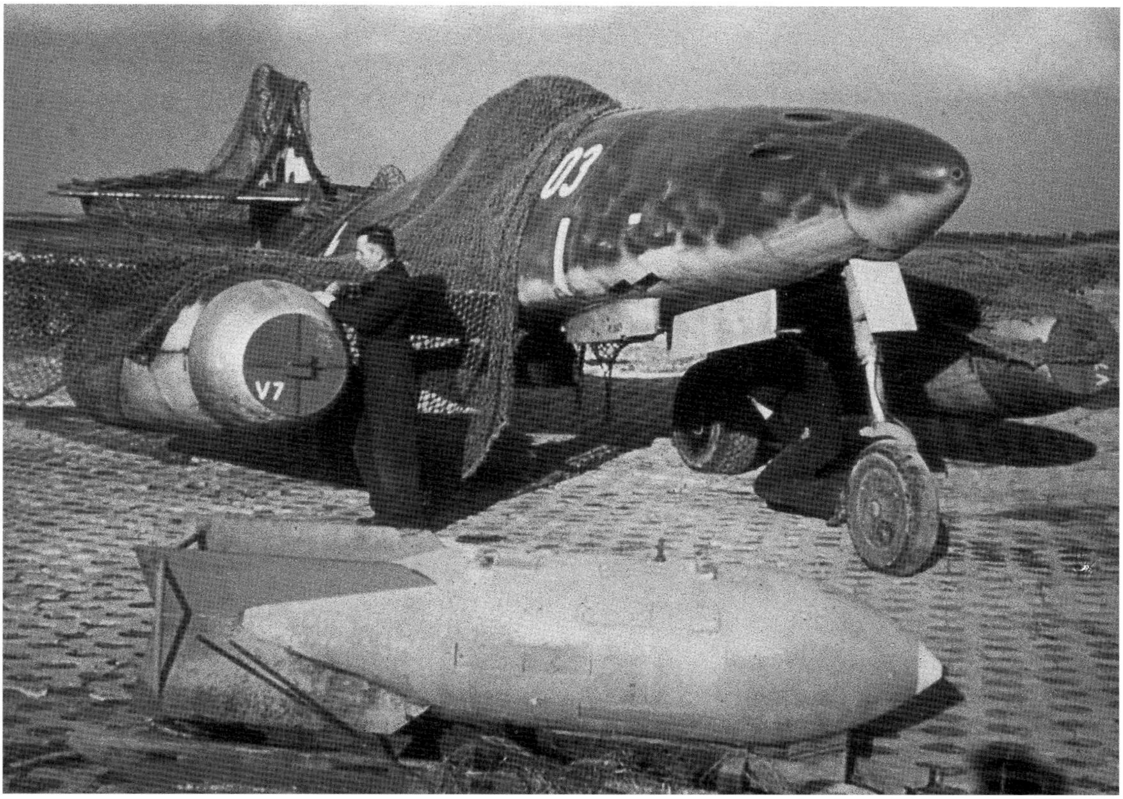
03
V7

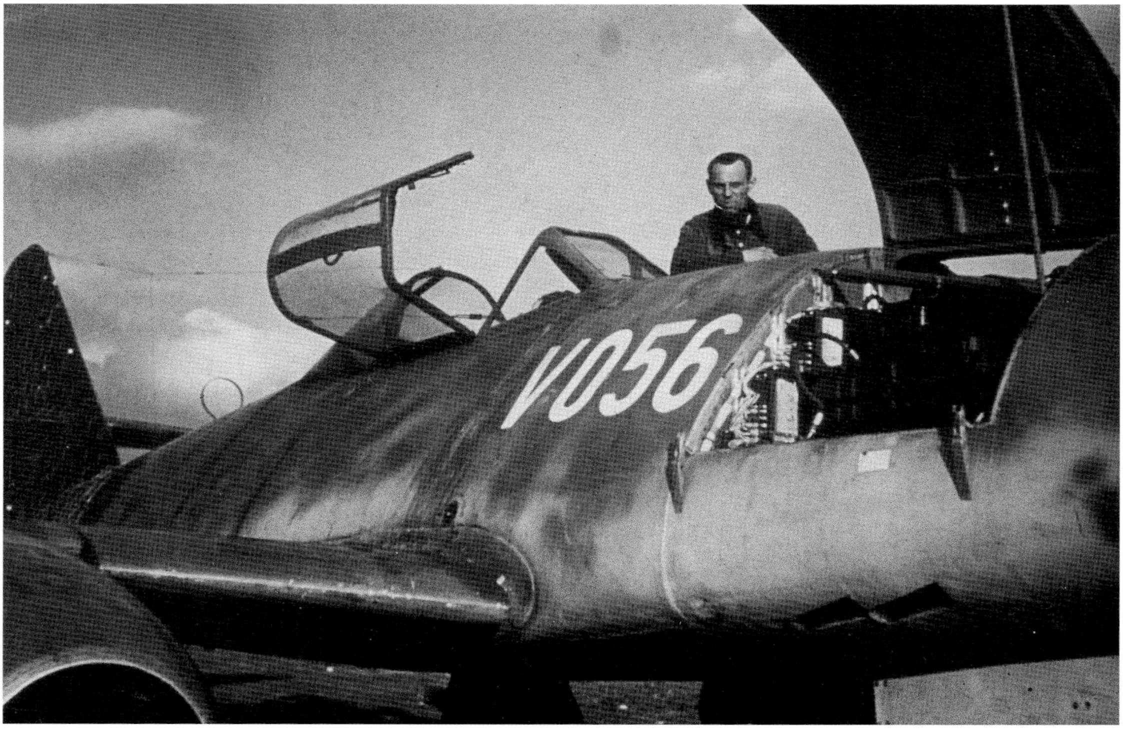
V056

Appendix 1:

Erprobungsverluste beim Kommando der Erprobungsstellen

ab 1927

Manufacturer	Aircraft type	Call sign	Works no.	Date
Arado	Ar SD 1	Unknown	0031	11/10/27
Albatros	L 76a	D-1127	10101	11/6/30
Messerschmitt	M 22	Unknown	0444	14/10/30
Albatros	L 78	Unknown	Unknown	4/3/31
Heinkel	HD 22c	D-1652	0307	4/5/31
Junkers	Ju 52 cai	D-2356	4005	27/5/33
Focke-Wulf	Fw 44a	D-2465	0155	5/9/33
Albatros	L 76	D-1283	10113	5/12/33
Klemm	Kl 35 V1	D-EHXE	0959	19/7/35
Klemm	Kl 35	Unknown	Unknown	17/1/36
Fieseler	Fi 98 V2	D-EBRA	1009	23/4/36
Junkers	Ju 86 V8	D-AVEE	6004	14/5/36
Junkers	W 34 hi	D-ONAN	0508	7/7/36
Heinkel	He 111 B-1	D-ARAU	1449	24/3/37
Henschel	Hs 123 V3	D-IKÓU	0267	1/4/37
Dornier	Do 23 G	D-ABOP	0352	27/4/37
Junkers	Ju 86 D-1	D-AOXE	0184	5/6/37
Messerschmitt	Bf 109 B-0	+2	1114	17/7/37
Boeing	247	D-AKIN	1944	13/8/37
Junkers	Ju 52 ge	D-AFYV	5352	23/11/37
Dornier	Do 217 V1	Unknown	0687	11/10/38
Messerschmitt	Bf 110 V7	D-AEDO	912	15/11/38
Junkers	Ju 90 V2	D-AIVI	4919	26/11/38
Henschel	Hs 126	D-IVHB	Unknown	6/2/39
Junkers	Ju 88 V9	D-ADCN	0001	31/3/39
Heinkel	He 111 P	D-AKFB	Unknown	23/5/39
Dornier	Do 17 M	D-AAQU	Unknown	24/6/39
Flettner	Fl 265 V3	TK+AN	1581	21/8/39
Junkers	Ju 88 A-4	Unknown	Unknown	22/2/40
Junkers	Ju 88 A-1	JD+IA	Unknown	26/2/40
Junkers	Ju 88 A-1	TP+AS	Unknown	13/3/40
Dornier	Do 17 M	GL+AT	2159	21/4/40
Heinkel	He 177 V3	D-AGIG	0003	24/4/40
Heinkel	He 111 H-4	TM+AS	6986	4/5/40
Heinkel	He 111 H-1	GQ+AC	Unknown	4/6/40
Heinkel	He 177 V2	CD+RQ	0002	27/6/40
Curtiss	H-75	1+2	Unknown	9/7/40
Klemm	Kl 35	GU+AM	Unknown	10/8/40
Focke-Wulf	Fw 58 C-1	GM+AZ	2099	28/8/40
Heinkel	He 118 V4	GQ+AJ	1963	2/9/40
Blohm&Voss	BV 142 V4	PZ+BD	0221	11/9/40
Arado	Ar 96 V6	GJ+AL	2069	26/9/40
Fieseler	Fi 156	Unknown	Unknown	5/11/40
Dornier	Do 17 M	GL+AT	2159	21/11/40
Junkers	Ju 87 B-1	GT+AT	0230	28/11/40
Henschel	Hs 129	Unknown	Unknown	16/12/40
Dornier	Do 215 B	CT+NA	2194	16/12/40
Junkers	Ju 87 R-1	PC+XV	5554	20/12/40
Dornier	Do 217 E-5	Unknown	Unknown	6/2/41

Place	Name	Remarks
Rechlin	Bienen, Dr.-Ing. Theodor (+)	Unknown
Smolensk	Künne und Thuy, Emil	Crashed on take-off
Augsburg	Mohnike, Eberhard	Crashed by Messerschmitt
Staaken	Kamecke, Peter von	Take-off accident (80%)
Staaken	Kamecke, Peter von u.a.	Damaged on take-off
Unknown	Bauer, Otto u.a.(inj.)	Emergency landing after engine fire
Rechlin	Rochow, Paul von	Crashed in a flat spin
Rechlin	Kneeser, Walter et al (+)	Crashed
Vietzen	König, Helmuth et al	Crashed due to surface failure
Waren	Jordan	Crashed due to insufficient height
Kassel	Schröder, Theo (+)	Ground loop
Meseritz	Heisig, Helmut et al	Crashed during range testing
Kempten	Anderssen, Harald et al (+)	Crashed due to bad weather
Triebsee/Pommern	Voelskow et al (+)	Crashed due to surface failure
Rechlin	Wulf, Heinz	Crashed
Leppinsee	Illigen, Werner et al (partial inj.)	Crashed after bombs detonated
Rechlin	Nagel, Adolf et al	Crashed after bombs detonated
Müritz	Jodlbauer, Dr. Kurt (+)	Crashed after flying accident
Hannover	Chun, Hans et al (+ und v)	Crashed on take-off
Roggentin	Medem, Ottokar Freihr.von (+)	Ground loop
Tettnang	Köppe, Dipl.-Ing. Rolf (+) et al	Crashed on a single-engine flight
Schwastorf	Nietruch, Friedrich Karl (+)	Collision with Ju 87 W34
Bathurst	Schwendler, Heinz et al(+)	Crashed on take-off
Rechlin	Grasmann et al	Emergency landing with damage
Rechlin	Moreau, Rudolf u. a.	Crashed during bombload evaluation
Rechlin	Grasmann et al	Damaged
Göhren	Lange, Willi et al	Ditched
Berlin-Schönefeld	Bay, Hans (+)	Crashed due to technical defect
Rambow	Glund, Hans-Ferdinand (+)	Crashed (automatic pilot)
Dessau	Grasmann et al	Crash-landing
Rechlin	Denecke, Herbert et al (+)	Crashed (dive-bomb sight)
Rechlin	Gembus, Erich (+) et al	Crashed after take-off
Gehlsdorf	Riekert, Hans-Friedrich et al (+)	Crashed during evaluation flight
Lärz	Wiesse, Hans et al (+)	Crashed (following railway line)
Prenzlau	Peters (+) et al	Crashed (engine fire)
Müritz-Graal	Ursinus, Fritjof (+) et al	Crashed during evaluation flight
Rechlin	Arlt, Werner (+)	Crashed on take-off
Rechlin	Böhm, Georg+Michael, Fritz (inj.)	Crashed (surface failure)
Schneeberg/Erzgb.	Meyer-Probst, Robert et al (+)	Ground loop
Rechlin	Ernst Udet	Crash-landing (10%)
Neustadt/Holstein	five civilians (+)	Crashed (100%)
Rechlin	No Injuries	Crash-landing (5%)
Rechlin	No Injuries	Damaged (30%)
Rechlin	Gembus (+)	Crashed on take-off
Schillersdorf	Maurer, Helmut et al (+)	Ground loop (flying accident)
Braunschweig	Balke, Hermann (+)	Crashed (instructional flight)
Rechlin	Hangleiter, Otto (+) et al (inj.)	Crash-landing after test flight
Schwarzenmoor	Othmer, Erich (+)	Crashed during dispersal flight
Lübben	One Civilian Injury	Crashed (95%) due to engine fire

Manufacturer	Aircraft type	Call sign	Works no.	Date
Dornier	Do 217 E-1	DD+LB	1002	3/3/41
Junkers	Ju 88 A-1	JB+RI	0065	14/3/41
Messerschmitt	Bf 109 E-1/B	Unknown	5813	15/3/41
Gotha	Go 242	Unknown	Unknown	18/3/41
Gotha	Go 242	Unknown	Unknown	26/4/41
Heinkel	He 111 H-6	Unknown	3780	10/5/41
Messerschmitt	Me 321	Unknown	0452	28/5/41
Messerschmitt	Bf 110 trop.	NM+IR	Unknown	4/6/41
Blohm&Voss	BV 138	Unknown	Unknown	9/6/41
Dornier	Do 217 C-0	D-ADBD	2710	4/7/41
Junkers	Ju 88 A-4	Unknown	1019	2/8/41
Heinkel	He 111 H-5	PH+EK	3921	31/8/41
Petlyakow	Pe 2			3/9/41
Heinkel	He 111 P-2	Unknown	2832	15/9/41
Messerschmitt	Bf 210 A-1	SJ+GG	0117	23/9/41
Messerschmitt	Bf 210 A-1	SJ+GI	0119	12/10/41
Dornier	Do 217 E-2	RB+YB	1180	22/10/41
Junkers	Ju 87 D-1	BK+ES	2019	7/11/41
Junkers	Ju 88 V11	GZ+AF	0003	24/12/41
Henschel	Hs 129 B-0	Unknown	0017	6/1/42
Siebel	Fh 104	Unknown	0039	11/1/42
Focke-Wulf	Fw 190 A-1	KB+PN	0012	20/1/42
Focke-Wulf	Fw 189	Unknown	Unknown	30/1/42
Heinkel	He 111 H-6	GA+SP	4206	8/2/42
Heinkel	He 177 A-07	GA+QP	0022	10/2/42
Heinkel	He 177 A-011	GA+QT	0026	17/2/42
Heinkel	He 177 A-06	GA+QO	0021	20/2/42
Heinkel	He 111 H-4	DC+BN	3239	26/2/42
Junkers	Ju 87 D-3	Unknown	2084	15/3/42
Gotha	Go 244	Unknown	22273	20/3/42
Heinkel	He 177 A-0	Unknown	Unknown	11/4/42
Messerschmitt	Bf 110 F-2	BD+WT	2658	28/4/42
Heinkel	He 177 A-02	DL+AQ	0017	6/5/42
Dornier	Do 217 E-2	RB+YD	1182	15/5/42
Siebel	Si 204 V3	Unknown	0003	1/6/42
Heinkel	He 177 A-0	DR+IT	32012	12/6/42
Gotha	Go 242	Unknown	Unknown	23/6/42
Dornier	Do 217 E-2	RH+EF	1132	24/6/42
Heinkel	He 177 A-0	GA+QW	0029	5/7/42
Junkers	Ju 52/3m	GT+AA	7455	5/7/42
Heinkel	He 177 A-0	Unknown	Unknown	16/7/42
Heinkel	He 177 A-013	GA+QV	0028	16/7/42
Focke-Wulf	Fw 190 A-3	DF+GM	0514	19/7/42
Messerschmitt	Bf 109 G-1	Unknown	14017	22/7/42
Messerschmitt	Bf 109 G-1	Unknown	14115	1/8/42
Dornier	Do 217 E-2	SK+WZ	1270	16/8/42
Junkers	Ju 87 V22	SF+TY	0540	20/8/42
Messerschmitt	Bf 109 G-1	Unknown	14019	22/8/42
Messerschmitt	Bf 109 G-1	Unknown	14020	29/8/42
Junkers	Ju 188 V3	GB+NF	Unknown	2/9/42
Heinkel	He 177 A-1	VE+UN	5214	5/9/42
Dornier	Do 217 M-01	BD+KO	1241	9/9/42
Dornier	Do 217 E-2	RB+GS	1197	12/9/42

Place	Name	Remarks
Rechlin	No Injuries	Crash-landing (75%)
Waltersdorf	unknown (+)	Crashed on take-off
Schönefeld	No Injuries	Crash-landing (40%)
Lärz	Thomas et al	Crash-landing (speed evaluation)
Bremen	Kirschke, Helmut et al (+)	Crash-landing (overland glider-tug flight)
Neustrelitz	Wittmann, Heinrich et al (+)	Crashed
Obertraubling	Flinsch, Bernhard et al(+)	Crashed (avionics)
Treviso	Baist, Walter (v)	Crash-landing
unbekannt	Reccius, Fritz et al (+)	Crashed (100%)
Gladau	Ostermaier, Adolf et al (+)	Crashed during blind-flying exercise
Krinke	Mallinckrodt, Friedrich von (+)	Crashed during evaluation flight
Mittelmeer	Lück, Rolf et al (+)	Missing
Müritz	Förschler, Friedrich (+)	Crashed on take-off
Chievres	No Injuries	Belly landing (20%)
Gut Ankershagen	Forgatsch, Heinz et al	Crashed (engine failure)
Rechlin	Madelung, Otto (inj.)	Crash-landing (95%)
Rechlin	Hasenclever, Ludwig et al(+)	Crashed (flaps and trim)
Neustrelitz	Parr, Josef (+), Bewerbung (inj.)	Ground loop on crash-landing
Riga-Spilve	No Injuries	Crash-landing (60%)
Rechlin	Bewermeyer, Konrad (+)	Crashed due to technical defect
Anklam	Two Civilian Injuries	Crashed (engine failure, 70 %)
Müritz	Steffen, Alfred (+)	Crashed
Gnesen	Jabzinski, Albert	Crashed
Müritz	Hannebohn, Werner (+) et al	Ground loop
unbekannt	No Injuries	Loss (90%)
Müritz	Wiegand, Heinrich et al (+)	Crashed due to engine fire
Deutsch Eylau	No Injuries	Damaged (5%)
Burg	Wiebe, Hans-Joachim (+)	Crashed due to engine fire
Drewitz	One Civilian Injury	Emergency landing (engine failure, 70%)
Danzig	No Injuries	Crash-landing (80%)
Rennes	Deutschmann, Hans et al (+)	Lost whilst with KG40
Zielow	Zeh, Albin et al (+)	Crashed as a result of engine failure
Rechlin	Baist, Walter (inj.)	Human error (20%)
Kraatz	No Injuries	Emergency landing (engine, 40%)
Buchholz	Trudrung, Max et al (+)	Crashed (avionics)
Rechlin	Schuch (inj.)	Crash-landing (70%)
Lärz	unknown (+)	Damaged whilst drogue-chute testing.
Nellingen	No Injuries	Tyre damage (60%)
Rechlin	No Injuries	Take-off accident (80%)
Rechlin	Two Civilian Injuries	Crashed (60%)
Rechlin	Gerds, Heinrich (+)	Crashed due to technical deficiencies
Malchow	Schiering, Otto (inj.) et al	Surface failure (100%)
Castel Benito	Elble, Franz (+)	Crashed during tropical performance evaluation
Lärz	No One Injured	Crashed after take-off (80%)
Bad Lausig	Schraps, Heinz (inj.)	Crashed (engine failure, 100%)
Roggentin	Kamp, Hans (inj.) et al	Crashed (engine failure)
Müritz	Rudhart, Hans (+)	Crashed (CO_2 poisoning)
Leussow	Leschhorn, Hans	Crashed
Angers	No Injuries	Crashed (engine failure, 20%)
unbekannt	unknown	Crashed (engine fire, 100%)
Müritz	Bayer, Gerhardt ua.	Crashed after tight turn
Müritz	Mann, Heinrich (inj.)	Crashed (65%)
Rechlin	Kloth, Fritz (inj.)	Crash-landing (engine, 60%)

Manufacturer	Aircraft type	Call sign	Works no.	Date
Messerschmitt	Bf 109 G-2	Unknown	4623	15/9/42
Junkers	Ju 88 A-4	BD+SF	1016	17/9/42
Grunau	Baby II a	Unknown	Unknown	1/10/42
Heinkel	He 111 H-6	CC+SE	4838	1/10/42
Dornier	Do 217 N-1	GG+YA	1401	11/10/42
Messerschmitt	Bf 109 G-2	CC+PF	14235	30/10/42
Siebel	Si 204 A-0	DI+IM	107144	3/11/42
Junkers	Ju 88	Unknown	Unknown	25/11/42
Messerschmitt	Bf 109 G-1	Unknown	77641	27/11/42
Junkers	Ju 52/3m	DG+KO	7565	2/12/42
Junkers	Ju 88 A-4	Unknown	140420	4/12/42
Dornier	Do 217 E-5	RE+CS	1119	8/12/42
Junkers	Ju 87 D-1	DK+EP	2016	8/12/42
Junkers	Ju 88 C-4	Unknown	0375	16/12/42
Heinkel	He 177 A-1	VE+UO	15215	21/12/42
Dornier	Do 217 E-2	RH+EO	1141	28/12/42
Heinkel	He 111 H-11	Unknown	5251	4/1/43
Heinkel	He 280 V1	NONE	280001	13/1/43
Dornier	Do 217 E-2	RH+EN	1140	26/1/43
Heinkel	He 177 A-3	ND+SK	35016	28/1/43
Focke-Wulf	Fw 190 V31	GH+KU	0056	29/1/43
Messerschmitt	Bf 109 G-2	BJ+WL	13515	5/2/43
Arado	Ar 232 A-01	VD+YA	0003	6/2/43
Junkers	Ju 88 D-1	BL+EU	1351	12/2/43
Focke-Wulf	Fw 190 A-4	Unknown	7189	3/3/43
Junkers	Ju 87	Unknown	2030	15/3/43
Dornier	Do 217 M-1	Unknown	51416	26/3/43
Messerschmitt	Bf 110 G-2	Unknown	5222	29/3/43
Junkers	Ju 88 P-1	Unknown	1398	19/4/43
Messerschmitt	Bf 110 G-3	DI+FE	4853	13/5/43
Dornier	Do 217 M-03	BD+KQ	1243	14/5/43
Dornier	Do 215 B-5	NO+TP	0066	14/5/43
Dornier	Do 215 B	Unknown	1405	15/5/43
Junkers	Ju 88	Unknown	Unknown	17/5/43
Heinkel	He 111 H-11	Unknown	7967	25/5/43
Messerschmitt	Bf 109 G-6	Unknown	15436	26/5/43
Heinkel	He 177 A-3	ND+SE	35010	2/6/43
Messerschmitt	Bf 108	Unknown	1995	11/6/43
Junkers	Ju 87	Unknown	1009	1/7/43
Siebel	Si 204	DI+IF	107137	20/7/43
Bücker	Bü 181	Unknown	0047	24/7/43
Focke-Wulf	Fw 190 A-5	Unknown	1405	28/7/43
Heinkel	He 111 H-6	CC+SZ	4859	10/8/43
Messerschmitt	Bf 109 E-7	CP+MY	3298	16/8/43
Gotha	Go 244	Unknown	886	19/8/43
Junkers	Ju 88 D-1	NF+KV	1587	19/8/43
Heinkel	He 177 A-3	Unknown	535365	23/8/43
Messerschmitt	Bf 109 G-6	Unknown	25644	31/8/43
Messerschmitt	Bf 109 G-2	Unknown	10830	6/9/43
Messerschmitt	Bf 110 F-2/trop.	CE+UI	4536	7/9/43
Focke-Wulf	Fw 190 A-3	Unknown	130270	10/9/43
Heinkel	He 177 A-3	GJ+RH	535446	15/9/43
Junkers	Ju 88 S-1	Unknown	0571	27/9/43

Place	Name	Remarks
Rechlin	No Injuries	Emergency landing (service flight, 40%)
Wittstock	Brose, Otto et al	Crashed
Stade	Kalbitzer, Edmund (+)	Crashed (human error)
Monte Veroli	Weichert, Erich et al (+)	Ground loop
Müritz	Ritter, Günther et al	Crashed
Demmin	Kaufmann, Egon (+)	Crashed (human error)
Bonn-Hangelar	Ernsting, Arnold et al (+)	Crashed (altitude sickness)
Latronico	Kalenzki, Georg et al	Crashed (technical deficiencies)
Lärz	No Injuries	Undercarriage damage (65%)
Mittelmeer	Schröder, Heinz et al	Missing whilst on delivery flight
Fahrenkrug	Bender. Wilhelm et al (+)	Crashed whilst on delivery flight
Taille-Fontaine	Jähnichen, Walter et al (+)	Crashed due to enemy action
Woterfitzsee	Fritz Albrecht et al (+)	Crashed during bombload evaluation
Rechlin	Koch, Claus, et al	Crashed during landing
Rechlin	unknown	Engine fire
Rechlin	Schober, Franz et al (inj.)	Belly landing (service flight)
München-Riem	No Injuries	Damaged (15%)
Lärz	No Injuries	Crashed (85%)
Mittelmeer	Walsch, Manfred et al	Missing on transport flight
Lärz	Blume, Eduard et al	Crashed after take-off
Rechlin	unknown	Crashed (100%)
Mirow	Willinger, Franz	Crashed after engine failure
Crossen a.d. Oder	Fieg, Paul et al (inj.)	Crashed (engine failure)
Rechlin	Voelcker, Kurt et al (+)	Crashed during emergency landing
Clemponow	Hartung, Heinz	Engine failure (80%)
Alt-Gaarz	No Injuries	Crashed (technical deficiencies, 100%)
Dessau	Kozian, Kurt (v)	Landing accident (35%)
Breslau-Schöngart.	No Injuries	Human error (15%)
Woterfitzsee	No Injuries	Crashed (100%)
Echterdingen	Grasmann et al	Engine failure (65%)
Kotzow	Sprung, Heinz et al (+)	Collision with Do 215 B
Kotzow	Werner, Helmut et al (+)	Collision with Do 217 M
Friedrichshafen	No Injuries	Crash-landing (80%)
Oberwiesenfeld	unknown	Crash-landing (25%)
unbekannt	No Injuries	Emergency landing (15%)
Rechlin	Knöfel, Horst (+)	Accident with Ju 87 on take-off
Buchholz	Koch. Hermann (inj.) et al	Crashed (bomb release mechanism)
Seehausen	No Injuries	Emergency landing (20%)
unbekannt	No Injuries	Crash-landing (20%)
Wittstock	Wabel, Rudi et al (inj.)	Emergency landing (engine, 75%)
Kunsche	NO INJURIES	Emergency landing (engine, 30%)
unbekannt	Fast, Helmut (+)	Missing when with *Erprobungskommando 25*
Kleve	Herzog, Dr., et al (inj.)	Crashed during evaluation flight
Cazeaux	Manthey, Alwin (+)	Crashed (100%)
Durach	Kaindel, Franz (inj.)	Emergency landing (engine, 65%)
Retzow	Pötzelberger, Josef et al (inj.)	Emergency landing (engine failure)
St. Raphael	No Injuries	Crash-landing (20%)
Rechlin	Gent, Wolfgang	Emergency landing (engine, 75%)
Rechlin	No Injuries	Human error (65%)
Müritz	Hesse, Werner et al (+)	Crashed during evaluation flight
Neu-Gaarz	Schmid, Lorenz (+)	Ground loop on crash-landing
Rechlin	Görlitz, Friedrich et al (inj.)	Crashed (technical deficiencies)
unbekannt	Frodl, Franz (inj.)	Damaged

Manufacturer	Aircraft type	Call sign	Works no.	Date
Dornier	Do 217 HV3	DD+LV	1023	28/9/43
Messerschmitt	Bf 110 E	Unknown	2655	29/9/43
Messerschmitt	Bf 109	GI+BW	Unknown	5/10/43
Messerschmitt	Bf 109 G	TR+GT	Unknown	8/10/43
Focke-Wulf	190 A-4	Unknown	140779	8/10/43
Messerschmitt	Bf 108	Unknown	2135	14/10/43
Messerschmitt	Bf 109 G	KL+ZV	27180	16/10/43
Junkers	Ju 88	Unknown	3218	19/10/43
Arado	Ar 79	unebk.	0029	20/10/43
Gotha	Go 244	VC+WC	0884	4/11/43
Heinkel	He 177 V19	VF+QA	332201	8/11/43
Heinkel	He 111	Unknown	0070	10/11/43
Heinkel	He 111 H-11	GL+ET	Unknown	10/11/43
Heinkel	He 111	Unknown	Unknown	20/11/43
Dornier	Do 17 Z	Unknown	2652	14/12/43
Heinkel	He 111 H-11	GL+EJ	110060	29/12/43
Heinkel	He 111 H-11	Unknown	8085	10/1/44
Heinkel	He 111 H-6	BE+KB	Unknown	27/1/44
Dornier	Do 17 Z	Unknown	3485	28/1/44
Heinkel	He 111 P-2	Unknown	2164	28/1/44
Fieseler	Fi 156 C-1	Unknown	110001	1/2/44
Dornier	Do 217	Unknown	Unknown	10/2/44
Messerschmitt	Bf 109 G-6	SU+XS	15435	24/2/44
Messerschmitt	Bf 110 G-4	Unknown	4860	26/2/44
Junkers	Ju 87 D-3	NJ+VZ	1260	1/3/44
Heinkel	He 111 P	Unknown	2168	3/3/44
Messerschmitt	Bf 110 G-2	PG+XJ	210010	6/3/44
Siebel	Si 204	Unknown	0012	13/3/44
Heinkel	He 111 H-6	Unknown	4989	14/3/44
Junkers	Ju 88 A-5	Unknown	3060	21/3/44
Heinkel	He 111 Z-1	Unknown	3225	26/3/44
Siebel	Si 204 V2	Unknown	0002	26/3/44
Focke-Wulf	Fw 190 A-5	Unknown	1180	27/3/44
Focke-Wulf	Fw 190 G-3	Unknown	160383	27/3/44
Dornier	Do 217 E-1	DD+LX	1024	27/3/44
Fieseler	Fi 156 C-1	Unknown	4286	27/3/44
Heinkel	He 111 H-11	Unknown	7536	27/3/44
Heinkel	He 111 H-6	Unknown	4432	27/3/44
Junkers	Ju 88 A-4	Unknown	2501	27/3/44
Junkers	Ju 88 A-4	Unknown	300024	27/3/44
Heinkel	He 219 V13	RL+AB	190052	28/3/44
Junkers	W 34	Unknown	4090	31/3/44
Messerschmitt	Bf 109 G-6	Unknown	160885	3/4/44
Dornier	DO 217 E-2	BK+IE	1216	5/4/44
Focke-Wulf	Fw 58	Unknown	Unknown	12/4/44
Heinkel	He 111	Unknown	Unknown	12/4/44
Junkers	Ju 87 D-3	Unknown	2452	12/4/44
Messerschmitt	Bf 109 G-6	GL+ZB	19210	13/4/44
Dornier	Do 335 V2	CP+UB	230002	15/4/44
Messerschmitt	Bf 109 G-6	Unknown	760078	19/4/44
Junkers	Ju 88	Unknown	39550	23/4/44
Arado	Ar 96 B-1	Unknown	4205	28/4/44
Heinkel	He 111 H-6	Unknown	7762	28/4/44

Place	Name	Remarks
Echterdingen	No Injuries	Crash-landing (10%)
Chatillon	No Injuries	Emergency landing (engine, 50%)
Rechlin	Baist, Walter (inj.)	Belly landing
Rechlin	No One Injured	Ground loop on landing
Altharm/Meppen	Mehlhorn, Kurt (+)	Air combat (ISS Focke-Wulf)
Arnstadt	No Injuries	Emergency landing (engine, 40%)
Wittstock	Heinig, Gottfried	Crashed
Staarken	No Injuries	Emergency landing (engine, 30%)
Rechlin	Crew (+) oder (inj.)	Crashed (engine failure, 90%)
Gotha	Schröder, Fritz et al	Crashed
Neustrelitz	Lippert, Meinhard et al (inj.)	Crashed (engine fire, 90%)
Toulouse	Gerlach, Helmut et al	Crashed during evaluation flight
Foggia	Unknown	Unknown
Jüterbog	Friebel, Walter (+)	Emergency landing due to weather
Stendal	No Injuries	Emergency landing (fuel, 80%)
Müritz	Wanninger, Hans et al (+)	Ditching
Aibling	No Injuries	Crash-landing (50%)
Rechlin	Sinram, Günter (inj.)	Damaged
Jatznich	No Injuries	Emergency landing (engine, 15%)
Damgarten	No Injuries	Emergency landing (30%)
Hof	No Injuries	Emergency landing (service flight, 80%)
Gießen	No Injuries	Crash-landing (15%)
Plauer See	Pohl, Rudolf	Shot down by enemy aircraft
Neustrelitz	Kucera, Walter et al (+)	Crashed (engine failure)
Hamburg	Stößel, Walter (+)	Emergency landing (engine fire)
Stargard	No Injuries	Crashed (100%)
Perleberg	Wachter, Ernst et al (inj.)	Shot down on active service
Rönne	No Injuries	Crashed (90%)
Wittenberg/Pomm.	No Injuries	Emergency landing (engine, 10%)
Insterburg	No Injuries	Technical deficiencies (15%)
Müritz	No Injuries	Belly landing (weather, 25%)
Karlshagen	No Injuries	Crashed during landing (100%)
Cazeaux	No One Injured	Enemy action (100%)
Cazeaux	No One Injured	Enemy action (25%)
Cazeaux	No Injuries	Enemy action (100%)
Cazeaux	No Injuries	Enemy action (100%)
Cazeaux	No Injuries	Enemy action (45%)
Cazeaux	No Injuries	Enemy action (100%)
Cazeaux	No Injuries	Enemy action (40%)
Cazeaux	No Injuries	Enemy action (100%)
Treptow	Jurk, Otto (+)	Crashed
Karlshagen	Bierwirtz, Karl et al (inj.)	Crashed on take-off (90%)
Karlshagen	Kykebush, Hans (inj.)	Ground loop (100%)
Faßberg	No Injuries	Enemy action (90%)
Vöslau	No Injuries	Enemy action (100%)
Vöslau	No Injuries	Enemy action (100%)
Vöslau	No Injuries	Enemy action (25%)
Schwinkendorf	Fischer, Herbert	Shot down on active service
Memmingen	Altrogge, Werner (+)	Crashed (engine fire)
Strehlen	No One Injured	Crash-landing (fog, 80%)
Unknown	Eiermann, August	Crashed during evaluation flight
Neustadt	No Injuries	Emergency landing (engine, 20%)
Karlshagen	No Injuries	Human error (60%)

Manufacturer	Aircraft type	Call sign	Works no.	Date
Flettner	Fl 223 V11	CI+SE	0011	5/5/44
Dornier	Do 17 M	RG+NW	2153	9/5/44
Junkers	Ju 88	VK+BW	Unknown	10/5/44
Junkers	Ju 88	Unknown	3218	10/5/44
Messerschmitt	Bf 109 G-6	VP+UT	Unknown	10/5/44
Heinkel	He 111 H-6	KI+XA	4093	21/5/44
Dornier	Do 17 Z	GL+AY	2517	21/5/44
Heinkel	He 111 H-16	Unknown	8208	24/5/44
Messerschmitt	Bf 109 E-2	Unknown	3934	30/5/44
Junkers	W 34	Unknown	1026	30/5/44
Heinkel	He 111 H-16	Unknown	4980	9/6/44
Heinkel	He 219 V26	Unknown	190120	11/6/44
Arado	Ar 232 B-010	QD+XP	110032	14/6/44
Heinkel	He 219 A-011	RL+AA	190061	16/6/44
Messerschmitt	Bf 110 G-4	TQ+LW	730023	22/6/44
Junkers	Ju 188 V2	Unknown	260141	22/6/44
Junkers	Ju 252 V6	DF+BR	0006	22/6/44
Junkers	Ju 87 D-5	BG+LW	130523	24/6/44
Dornier	Do 217	Unknown	Unknown	25/6/44
Focke-Wulf	Fw 190 G-3	Unknown	160421	29/6/44
Junkers	Ju 88 V41	DE+KD	5002	1/7/44
Heinkel	He 111 H-5	Unknown	3949	19/7/44
Arado	Ar 234 S1	GM+BA	140101	25/7/44
Heinkel	He 111 H	Unknown	2502	31/7/44
Bücker	Bü 181	Unknown	0888	16/8/44
Henschel	Hs 130 A-0	GM+OQ	130005	5/9/44
Henschel	Hs 130 E-0	CF+OX	130054	5/9/44
Messerschmitt	Me 262 A-1	E3+03	170038	5/9/44
Junkers	Ju 88	Unknown	340083	11/9/44
Junkers	Ju 188 E-1	Unknown	260308	17/9/44
Focke-Wulf	Fw 190 D-9	TR+SD	210004	25/9/44
Messerschmitt	Me 323 V16	DU+QZ	130211	30/9/44
Arado	Ar 234 B-2	GM+BP	140116	12/10/44
Focke-Wulf	Fw 190	Unknown	Unknown	27/11/44
Arado	Ar 234 S17	GM+BQ	140117	7/12/44
Arado	Ar 234 S4	GM+BD	140104	18/12/44
Messerschmitt	Me 262 A-1	SQ+XA	130188	2/2/45
Arado	Ar 234 B-2/N	SM+FE	140145	13/2/45
Focke-Wulf	Ta 152	CW+CH	150008	20/2/45
Messerschmitt	Me 262 A-1	Unknown	110466	22/2/45
Messerschmitt	Me 262 A-1	Unknown	110967	22/2/45
Fieseler	Re 2	NONE	Unknown	5/3/45
Junkers	Ju 52/3m	PB+UA	Unknown	16/4/45
Junkers	Ju 52/3m	GC+BK	Unknown	17/4/45
Arado	Ar 234 C	Unknown	Unknown	26/4/45
Messerschmitt	Me 262 A-1	Unknown	Unknown	27/4/45
Albatros	L 47b	D-586	Unknown	19/10/26
Albatros	L 76a	Unknown	10106	22/7/27
Albatros	L 77	D-1547	10137	6/3/29
Albatros	L 76	D-1210	10111	13/6/29
Focke-Wulf	Fw 190	Unknown	5226	Unknown
Henschel	Hs 129 B-1	Unknown	0154	Unknown

Place	Name	Remarks
Bösel	Gerstenhauer, Hans-H. (inj.)	Crash-landing (35%)
Lärz	Dührkop, Karl (+) et al	Crashed during landing
Vietzen bei Rechlin	Baist, Walter	Crash-landing (single engine)
Oberwiesenfeld	No Injuries	Human error (20%)
Rechlin	Sinram, Günter (inj.)	Abandoned take-off and crash-landed
Minden	Beck, Georg et al (+)	Collision with Do 17 Z
Minden	Mann, Eberhard et al (+)	Collision with He 111 H6
Großenrbrode	No Injuries	Undercarriage damage (25%)
Zwischenahn	No One Injured	Enemy action (20%)
Zwischenahn	No Injuries	Enemy action (100%)
Karlshagen	No Injuries	Undercarriage damage (50%)
Prag-Rusin	Leudes, Helmut et al (+)	Crashed (100%)
Lärz	Goedicke, Theo (+.) et al	Crashed (technical deficiencies)
Mirow	Huß, Karl-Heinz et al(+)	Crashed following avionics damage
München	Behrmann, Günter (+)	Crashed whilst with de-icing *Kommando*
Dessau	No Injuries	Collision with Ju 252 V6
Dessau	No Injuries	Collision with Ju 188 V2 (20%)
Kemijärvi	Hildebrand, Fritz et al (+)	Crashed (human error)
Mielec	Rose, Angst, Schneider (inj.)	Emergency landing (engine, 70%)
Nellingen	No One Injured	Undercarriage damage (10%)
Rechlin	Borsdorff, Heinz	Belly landing (undercarriage)
Schleißheim	No Injuries	Enemy action (20%)
Lärz	Lissau, Herbert (+)	Ground loop on take-off
Schongau	No Injuries	Enemy action (90%)
Dessau	No Injuries	Enemy action (10%)
Echterdingen	No Injuries	Enemy action (100%)
Echterdingen	No Injuries	Enemy action (90%)
Lärz	Ruther, Johann (+)	Crashed
Fürth	Zeitter, Ernst et al	Ground loop on landing
Schillerdorf	Dietz, Friedrich et al	Crashed (human error)
Roggentin	Thoenes, Alexander (+)	Ground loop during landing
Heuberg	Poping, Herbert et al (+)	Crashed during parachute evaluation
Lärz	Arndt, Hans-Egon (inj.)	Collision with obstacle on take-off
Roggentin	Neidhart, Karl-Gustav (+)	Crashed (CO2 poisoning)
Lärz	Kunz, Jakob	Crashed during evaluation flight
Burg	Unknown (+)	Crashed during landing
Lärz	Furchner, Hans	Crash following TL damage
Oranienburg	Bisping, Josef et al (+)	Crashed (100%)
Rechlin	Baist, Walter	Belly landing in a field
Lärz	Unknown	Loss (100%)
Lärz	Unknown	Loss (20%)
Buchholz	Stabati, Walter	Crashed (structural failure)
Mecklenburg	Hausmann, Walter et al	Shot down by fighter-bomber
Neu-Wustrow	Piatschek, Joachim et al	Shot down by enemy aircraft
Lechfeld	Abels, Hans-Joachim (+)	Crashed after TL failure (take-off)
Oberpfaffenhofen	Gebel, Kurt	Crash-landing (ground loop)
Adlershof	Seefeld, Max	Crashed as a result of over-use
Berlin-Rudow	Mühlhan, Fritz et al	Crashed in a flat spin
Kotzow	Arens, Hans	Crashed due to structural failure
Kotzow	Jeschonnek, Dr. Paul	Crashed pulling out of reverse loop
Unknown	No Injuries	Loss (40%)
Rechlin	No Injuries	Lost after fire (85%)

Where the symbol (+) appears, this is the German way of denoting that the pilot and possibly accompanying aircrew were killed in the associated event.

Appendix 2:

Erprobungskommandos

(Evaluation units of the Luftwaffe)

Erprobungskommando 4	Evaluation of the X-4-missile
Erprobungskommando 9	Unknown aluation purposes
Erprobungskommando 15	Evaluation of Hs 293 the glide-bomb
Erprobungskommando 16	Evaluation of the Me 163 fighter
Erprobungskommando 1	X- and Y-wireless systems
Erprobungs- und Lehrkommando 18	Carrier-based aircraft
Erprobungskommando 19	Tropical evaluation
Erprobungs- und Lehrkommando 20	Carrier-based aircraft
Erprobungs- und Lehrkommando 21	Evaluation of the PC1400X-bomb
Erprobungs- und Lehrkommando 22	Evaluation of the Fw 190 as fighter/bomber
Erprobungs- und Lehrkommando 24	Evaluation of navigation systems
Erprobungskommando 25	Evaluation of rocket installations
Erprobungskommando 26	Evaluation of anti-tank weapons
Erprobungskommando 36	Evaluation of the Hs 293 weapon
Erprobungskommando 40	Spraying of insecticide
Erprobungskommando 41	Spraying of insecticide
Erprobungskommando 100	X- and Y-wireless systems
Erprobungskommando Ta 152	Operational evaluation of the Ta152
Erprobungskommando Ta 154	Operational evaluation of the Ta154
Erprobungskommando He 162	Operational evaluation of the He162
Erprobungskommando Ar 234	Operational evaluation of the Ar234
Erprobungskommando Me 262	Operational evaluation of the Me262
Erprobungskommando Do 335	Operational evaluation of the Do335
Erprobungskommando Ju 388	Operational evaluation of the Ju388
Erprobungskommando Kolb	Unknown evaluation purposes
Erprobungskommando Nebel	Evaluation of the Me264 aircraft

Erprobungsstaffeln

(Evaluation squadrons of the Luftwaffe)

Erprobungsstaffel Ju88	Tactical evaluation of the Ju88 A-1
Erprobungsstaffel Me109 G	Tactical evaluation of the Bf109 G-1
Erprobungsstaffel He177	Tactical evaluation of the He177 A-1
Erprobungsstaffel Ju188	Tactical evaluation of the Ju188
Erprobungsstaffel Fw190	Tactical evaluation of the Fw190
Erprobungsstaffel Me210	Tactical evaluation of the Me210
Erprobungsstaffel Me410	Tactical evaluation of the Me410
Transportstaffel 40	Tactical evaluation of helicopters